DOUBLE TRIO 3

NERVE CHURCH

DOUBLE TRIO 3

NERVE CHURCH

NATHANIEL MACKEY

A New Directions Paperbook Original

Some of these poems first appeared in the following publications: *Almost Island, BOMB Magazine, The Carolina Quarterly, Conjunctions, Decoded: A Duke Performances Journal, Exhibit A, Granta: The Magazine of New Writing, Gulf Coast: A Journal of Literature & Fine Arts, Hambone, Here, Kenyon Review, New American Writing, The Oxford American, Poetry, The Tusculum Review, The Vassar Review, The Yale Review.*

The author and publisher would like to thank the Humanities Division of Trinity College of Arts and Sciences at Duke University and selva oscura press for their generous support of this publication.

Manufactured in the United States of America
First published as volume three of *Double Trio* in 2021
Design by Eileen Bellamy

Library of Congress Cataloging-in-Publication Data
Names: Mackey, Nathaniel, 1947- author.
Title: Double Trio / Nathaniel Mackey.
Description: New York, NY : New Directions Books, 2021. |
Series: Double Trio – Tej Bet ; So's Notice ; Nerve Church
Identifiers: LCCN 2020043509 | ISBN 9780811230629 (set)
Subjects: LCGFT: Poetry.
Classification: LCC PS3563.A3166 D68 2021 | DDC 811/.54—dc23
LC record available at https://lccn.loc.gov/2020043509

10 9 8 7 6 5 4 3 2

New Directions Books are published for James Laughlin
by New Directions Publishing Corporation
80 Eighth Avenue, New York 10011

ndbooks.com

for Joseph Donahue

and

in memory of Wilson Harris
1921–2018

        now it is certain that water
is a magical substance.   it will drink
up all things.   and I am told this is
most like love, who stood near the
high way, and because it is one of
the few bare places the world has
ever known, love asked directions,
but the high way ran on.   now it is
certain that the high way is a magical
substance.   it will lead inside the
shape of things.

—Robin Blaser, *The Holy Forest*

And it seemed to me as I listened I had understood that no living ear
on earth can truly understand the fortune of love and the art of victory
over death without mixing blind joy and sadness and the sense of
being lost with the nearness of being found.

—Wilson Harris, *Palace of the Peacock*

CONTENTS

I
RUM

ANUNCIO'S ELEVENTH LAST LOVE SONG

—"mu" one hundred ninetieth part—

I awoke in a room filled with sound,
morning sun, reminiscent bouquet my
   mind's intoxicant. A whiff of Anuncia's
                              loin-
musk all it took, heaven looked at from afar
   but in sight, attar's near rhyme I persuaded
   myself... Rose petals where legs met, love
                              lore
   had it once, a synaptic transit we gave the
      name tej bet we gave a new name, refugee
dismay we called it now. Fugitive ambit we
   named it as well, a throwdown sound were it
                              a
matter of sound, threnodic by its light, jump
   summons by everything else's, ankles the
   texture of tree trunks, ants crawling our feet...
                              Keep
   walking was the music's advice, fugitive mu-
sic, two muses, one bitter, one sweet. Synaptic
   transit's alchemical attitude sulfurous, complaint
                              ever
   about to break out. It might've been a pike's
jaw lyre we plucked, it might've been shaken
   sleep needles gave off sound. No doubt we were
a band, we banded together, no way were we not.
                              Either
   way we were a band, just two of us no matter,
      music a shared mustiness or musk we lay en-
tranced in, the smell of our hands out from up each
   other's legs we'd never get over, no last love song
                              we
   sang... But got over it, planet banality we said,
only what could be would be. "Let's not and say
   we will," we announced at every turn, advancing
                              the
virtuality of things. "What could've been would've
   been," we were chanting even so. Anuncia broke
   her tooth on a grain of sand eating mussels. Two
                              two-

headed eagles, two hoodoo birds, bore down on
us. Leg half-dead, I knew notice had been served.
    Planet banality went exactly so, caught not by cap-
ture but cloth put out we looked at, wondering what

                                                    lay
    underneath. Fold had its way with us, wrinkle had
    its way, whatever spirited teeth took tongue to them-
selves, whatever broken teeth took up... We were in

                                                    Italy
    next thing we knew, reckoning the walls of the city,
Salento's charismatic scrum's lab sentiment, tantric
    or tarantistic we couldn't say. Lipsmear ran them as

                                                    one,
    a corked bottle's containment let loose, catechrestic
smack, world virtuality afoot. Lipsmear's correction
    said to be shown in heaven, in heaven were heaven to

                                                    be
    had... No ideal but that hers was hers, mine mine,
    soon-come consonance the work of who knew what, bits
    arrayed at last as they would be... A loose confeder-
acy of sorts not to be messed with, polis meant wall we

                                                    knew.
    "Took between teeth and lips" the wording that came
to mind, hers nor my style to be so roused or to get up-
    set, sex-polis's long odds against polis lost on no one, the

                                                    sha-
    dow Nub cast every-
where

Anuncia knew what we were doing more than she
   knew, more than she would say she knew, more than
she could say. We put our heads together, no longer
                                             bound
      by *The Book of So*, inconsequence consequence's
jam from there on, love's long mystical demeanor
   no sooner let go… What did it want to say that we
                                             were
      there bidding it goodbye we wondered, the last love
         song we didn't sing we were singing, we who made no
claim on beauty, no claim to be beautiful, the beauti-
   ful neither come nor soon come. We stood buffeted by
                                             what
      beauty might be, beauty neither the point nor beside it,
   what repair there was no longer the point… "Tell me, tell me,
   tell me," we broke out blabbing, each at the end of the day a
                                             low
      cheek to hold
on to

•

We let time have its way, as if otherwise were
an option, time tolling life beyond capture.
Tenuous kin what kin were available, always

ever

to make of it more than it was, pits in our
gouged-out torsos given the look of abalone
shells. Rock on light's illusory buttress, Anun-
cia's promise it seemed... World virtuality all

there

was of it to revert to, no site for which would
occur or to which appearance could accrue, the
drape of her gown the obduracy of stone. I was

trying

to float a sense of intent, the point at which it
all arrived a leap, then a letdown, wondering was
all it was all there was, wondering was there

any-

thing more... Was it only the pull of her bis-
cuit brought me she wondered out loud, only the
smell of it what thrall there was. We were no He-
len and Achilles run aground in Egypt, we spoke

our

minds. We nakedly said what arrested us, no
cloth obscured our truth. Better biscuit be where
we meet, I rebutted, than biscuitless we meet no-
where at all. No hawk flew by, no glove's iron grip,

we

were the far side of that... My biscuit her biscuit,
I rebutted, hers mine. Nothing broke leaving us no-
where. Sand, it seemed, stuck to our feet, no matter.

It was

no Egyptian beach we were on. Her biscuit my bis-
cuit, mine hers. Her calling her biscuit the only one,
wanting me to call it the onliest one, voice cut from

bur-

lap it seemed. Voice brought of burlap edged in
raw silk, bright scree of light off the doctor's daugh-
ter's teeth, Anuncia the doctor's daughter again,

the

girl she'd been be-
fore

One last biscuit time, moment's token, mo-
　　ment promising more than moment. Moment
we'd been about before unbeknown to us,
　　　　　　　　　　　　　　　　　one
　　last, lost biscuit time night's proffer, prof-
　　fer part boon, part predicament, bewitch-
ment, what but when it was, what but what it
　　　　　　　　　　　　　　　　　want-
　　ed, reach no end of which bore fruit, blue
plunder, whence it would always be… The
　　promise of it sweeter than the it of it, one last
　　　　　　　　　　　　　　　　　　or
　　one lost biscuit time's attainment. Love's de-
liberative wont. Love's disconsolate assay. Love's
　　last caroling soon come, sweet proffer, the it
　　　　　　　　　　　　　　　　　of
　　it the what of it, it wanted to be known, giving
　　　　　　　　　　　　　　　　　us
　　its we to
keep

—brother b's roman sojourn—

Brother B gathered his locks, bound
   them with a tie at the back of his head.
The ponytail made his head a horse's

                     ass
   he proclaimed. He'd gone on a trip
and just gotten back. The place he'd
   been he called Rum… Next we knew

                    he
said he came out of a Capuchin crypt,
   Brother Bone of late, a bite of sound's im-
   position on the air. A bite of sound's

                   phi-
   losophic insistence, he said. A philo-
sophic bone recital, he said, bent on
   giving one pause. A philharmonic non-
sonance, he said, gave him pause… The

                pony-
   tail, he repeated, made his head a horse's
   ass. Don't say that, we begged, hit by
wisdom's idiocy, the wisdom of the idiots

               his.
   We'd begun to be won over, a demonic
or a divine cartoon we were in, so quick
   it made our heads twist off. A two-headed

              eagle
   had us hoodoo'd, he said, a bite of sound
on the air Nub's ancestry, Nub's predecessor
   address… Once again, he said, the call was

             to
   love our captors, love them though we did
   and got nothing, offer up another cheek. He
was talking out of his head but we heard him,

           his
   head a horse's ass but what he said stayed
with us, what he said sort of tell-my-horse.
   Romulus choked Uncle Remus, he said, what

          he

meant by which was worldly Rum, he went
on to explain, the lesson of ruin all over. By
   that he meant to say, he went on to explain,
went on to ask, monument packed on monument

                                          mean-

   ing what. Quick blood and bone come to naught,
      he went on to say, was what he meant, Rum's
feted mortality eternal… Mrs. Fret said had no busi-
   ness there in the first place, picked her own bone,

                                       phi-

losophic herself. Brother B paid her no mind. Be-
   ing back made it feel like a dream, he said, a
   dream he not so much dreamt as he was dreamt

                                          by,

   the dream, he raised his voice insisting, dreamt
him. A glad sadness came over us hearing him,
   sound spilled out of our book. What he said we

                                       saw,

      copacetic witnesses, arms and legs rickety
sticks with a leak of spirit, this or that bodily pre-
   cinct, he said, owned by a Mr. Hot Pot… An
old song was on the box, the box's ubiquity all we

                                          had,

   the box more book than box. So it came to be
      Mrs. Vex held her tongue, the music's wounded
voice, infectious, invaded hers, his and her spit's
   benediction, tongue's touch of tongue immaculate

                                          still.

   All it was was that Rum still stood, ruin's eternity,
all it was was that ruin stood still… Brother B was
   back, it seemed he never left, he said, his wandering

                                          eye

   the music's way-
ward kin

(chorus)

It was song number four times fifty-seven
  but no one was counting. Brother B spoke of
there being more days in Rum than he could
                              say,
     more the more he remembered but more
than he could remember, a stone cabin perched
on a stilt where the wind blew thru, Mr. Hot
                         Pot's
     calipers made in heaven... He dreamt he lay
on the floor looking up Mrs. Vex's dress, her
  "had no business there in the first place" pure
seduction, all of it amid stone unthinkably old.
                              What
     to say, what to say, we yelled out, an insurgent
       sneeze kept at bay inside our noses, twin pinch-
     es of next-level snuff up each of our nostrils, our
                                   copa-
     cetic witness in-
     tact

•

Rum, Brother B said, turned his head, his
     head a horse's ass after the fact. A horse's
     ass after his own heart, he said, mule as
                              much
     as horse, he said. Rum fell away from
the tips of his toes, brick-brown expanse at
     the foot of the hill his cabin sat hoisted
on. A bamboo stilt, he said, beginning to be
                              out
     of breath, a board or a bamboo stilt stone's
     rescue, stone's mortality rehearsed... It
was idiot wisdom. We wanted away from it.
                              We
     wanted in, we wanted out, a conflicted choir,
          copacetic witness's relay. Brother B's way of
saying Rome made it Antillean, a move he in-
     vited us in with and we followed, heads ridden
                              hard
as his. Rum was on the ground but of the air, he
     said, bamboo bent by the storm that blew thru.
     He took refuge in the Capuchin basement, he
                              said.
     We tilted our heads, high-pitched, a birdhead-
     ed breed of horse... It was tell-my-horse talk
     we took it. Brother B wasn't really there. Rum
said it as well as Rome, he was right. Rome wasn't
                              real-
     ly there. Rome undone the day he got there, he said,
     Rum run come in a day. Ruin's weaponized we,
he said, seed of empire, a dead horse left in his bed,
                              he
     said, neigh not letting
go

(chorus)

Rum plied fact, feeling, the smell of whose
rooms an obtuse heaven. He stood ingesting
   the bones' memo, gratuitous memo. Bone

                            re-
cognizes bone, he said. Ruin, he said, was
   Rum's middle name, trigger, tripwire, fin-
   ger, its own whatever came after, all that

                             came
   after… All the he-said, we'd have said, a
kind of tell-my-horse, horse's-ass-headed as
   he was, birdheaded as were we, a miracle

                             of
the fishes with nary a fish in sight. We'd've
   said horse's-ass-headed, we'd've said nary,
   buoyed by the feel of each on our tongues,

                          copa-
cetic witness run
come

Brother B had us imagining a stone cot-
    tage atop a bamboo stilt, the monks' gra-
tuitous reminder everlasting ruin, everlast-
ing Rum… Meanwhile back in Nub we
                                    were
    no longer athwart our skin, hot anger
    blown down our necks no matter, hot anger
    white hot, white anger, white complaint,
                                        comb-
    over's would-be
Rum

SECOND ÉTUDE ENDING "SOON COME" REBEGUN

—"mu" one hundred ninety-second part—

He lay hoisted high, oliloqui's hit under-
way, Andreannette's waist and midriff
magnetic, his arm forever around her it
                                            seemed.
   Andreannette, the thought of the backs
of whose legs waylaid him, the thought
of whose thigh crossing his cut deep, An-
dreannette, the thought of whose heft. She
                                            of
   the short hair, she of the billowing pea
    coat, his and her bodily regret no matter,
her big-tent body blessed... As would be
                                            his,
   hers willing, torn sky, rolled-away rock,
eyelids thin like rice paper, kissed and ca-
   ressed bodily amends. "We be saying things
we don't mean," the muses whispered, exactly
                                            the
   way, he lay thinking, Hesiod said. He lay flat
   but with a head for figures, twelve squared
minus thirty-one a feel for woundedness, eros
   touching on elegy, wear, something of a sculp-
   tor's touch... He forgot his name, so caught
                                            up
   he got to be. He lay remembering Trane not
knowing who Willie Mays was, head in a cloud
   of sound, sound itself a cloud, head itself as
                                            well,
   inside a head of sound. He lay thinking how
    virtual it all was, him with a feel for numbers,
a cloaked or a cloistered world, aboveness's re-
   gret... Such to be his way, the thought of it the it
                                            of it,
   short of it no matter, soon
come

•

He lay bumped up with a feel for numbers,
three hundred eighty-six divided by two. "Touch
while we can," he lay thinking, the sun's blue

camp-

fire caught in the tree limbs. "Touch while
we can," he kept telling himself. He thought
thought a kind of touch, touch thought, hands

not

hands only in thought not inexpert, each all over
the other due thought… He and she all over
each other he thought, himself more virtual the

long-

er he thought, touch's confirmation thought's
prop. She too found her body's defeat virtual,
eventual, all the more reason to hold on, all the
more to let go, the this of it gone to some that of

it,

whatever touch was, buttressing thought. The
sandpaper feel of his ankles, the low fold of her
belly, her waist, the weight of the earth in the sag

of

their skin… So again it was a lay of the lifted.
He and she lay hoisted skyward, backs to the
ground. Sinew and gristle pop reconnoitered Brother
B's bone show, mortality made muse, reminder.

Rem-

iniscent kiss, reminiscent caress, recalling having
once been young, the great conundrum what to do
with it gone with it gone, he and she touched while

they

could

Silhouettes were all they were, said one school
of thought, looked at from outside quickening
memory, figures in a dimly lit room. All they
                                                    were
were outlines, dark all they were, the Cape
Verdean gallop heard in back their wedding
song, outlines darkened in. Outline and dark
                                                    alone
discernible, body not to be trusted they'd been
taught... Was it Eleanoir come back in a dream
he wondered, in a dream or as if in a dream he
                                                    won-
dered, each the insistence of dream they'd been
taught. Was it Itamar come back, she wondered,
he and she allies of late of the dead's brigade,
                                                    meta-
physical what-for and wont not to be negated,
was it Itamar come back in a dream or as if in a
dream... "Touch while we can" came up again. No
way did having said it already say it, "We be saying
                                                    things
we don't mean" said again
as well

•

They'd gone over to the shadow side, things
   going on inside she couldn't see, things going
on he couldn't see. The moot luxuriance of
                           be-
   fore drew them in tow, lost elixir, lost lap-
is, gloom's alchemical body its own it of it, on-
   liness let breath be their mat. "Breath, be our
                           mat,"
   they heard themselves whisper, gloom's ad
hoc receipt having none of it, heard it, taken out
   of themselves... Nursed grudges... Moodi-
ness's remand... They were gloom's Ethiopians,
                           yet
   to assume new names, alchemy's gloom gloom's
   alchemy, a circle they lay unable to get out of.
Night had come again in Low Forest. It now came
                       again
   on Lone Coast, alchemy's vitriolic wish their
   one hope, sulfuric sun said to be locked in the
   dark... The night's cry went by the book, all as
                     had
been prophesied, prophecy's fulfillment rote, their
   book an asthmatic horn's adornment, mat what lit-
tle breath were there breath. There was a droning
                   low
   tone thought itself made it seemed, the erotics
of it less than obvious, gloom's day dark as night.
   Though the study of it said otherwise, boded blankly,
what-to-say-so-to-say bordered on "We be saying...,"
                   they
   so touched and were so taken out... What was left
   of what we saw we who stood looking on no longer
saw, deep study colluded with by dark study. "Know
that it's not really me," they now said to each other,
                   we
   could hear but not see, breath but whatsaid gospel
were there breath and there was breath, whatsaid re-
sumption of love or its replacement, intimacy quick
                   with

   disar-
ray

————————————————

Soon-come came and went, universal exhaust,
    universal dead heat. Built up to more build-
up, only more buildup, onliness's bumptious

                                    re-
    set. We called it a wondrous restoration, res-
titution, snide choir, bitten by love's replace-
    ment's bug, horned ornaments, armature what

                                        held
        us at bay… They were the two each of whose
    heaven was to inhale the other's bodily attar,
        his to inhale hers, hers to inhale his, each their
    own scent up close off the other. They were the

                                        snide
        bride and the snide bridegroom, piss and per-
    fume, design each on the other so thick we could
        smell it, pinched alchemical wedding, still in

                                        the
    dark

•

Their heads their sole houses they'd been
   taught, school of what hit, school of
what hurt, an abacus of knots and bumps.
                                    Mr.
   P's bug eyes were their eyes as they
      strained in the dark, the moon's dilated
light far away outside. Mr. and Mrs. P of
                                 late,
   Amadou and Andreannette, Odudua's
eastern sky something seen in a face no face
   avowed, failing it their bodies' compromise…
Mr. P's memo regarding what counted came
                                 and
   went, song one hundred six and a half times
      two, song seventy-one times nine divided
by three, song seventeen hundred four divided
                                 by
eight. What counted were polls that were clouds
   darkening the sky, gloom they were taught
would spur gold. We were hearing poll and we
                                 were
   hearing pall… An exchange consorting inside
and out, votes cast curbside floated out to sea,
   ballots folded up into paper boats. Paper boats
were Junkanoo headdress, paper hats, our heads
                                 float-

   ed out to
sea

We woke up scared, we put King Pleasure
  on the box. Either we were looking in
or they were looking out. No way, we told

                                    our-
   selves, could it be both... There was a
  we, there was a they, as always, wish or
    exhort it otherwise though we did. That it
was that way had grown more somber, our

                                 lopped
   heads' ythmic roll... We were afraid we
  were back in Nur, Nub's new name ass-back-
   wards, Bun, Kronos's golden field wasted,

                            the
  comb-over scythe come
thru

"Sacred drift, sacred midriff," he had said
   seeing Andreannette approach, always
   the heralded elsewhere, dreamt unrest no

                                    re-
   solve could dispatch... Gloom's alche-
      my lay like low-lying mist, clung to the
   contours of the ground they reminisced,
      lost ground yet to be let go. Andreannette's

                                    big-
      ness an earth unto itself he fantasized...
      Redeemed everydayness... Self a kind of soil

                                    re-
   worked

It was after the rain with no rainbow. The
   rainbow dried up, wept before it went,
white grievance had hold of it we heard.
                                             We
   weren't traveling, we were being chased
      it turned out, the bullet holes in Amadou's
body come back to instruct us, Andrean-
   nette's inconsolate kiss. We ran amending

                                        our
   slave state sutra, endlessly extended it
seemed… The little books we had were all
   we had, little books we made pressing
our tongues to the backs of our teeth. What

                                        was
   timbre, we wanted to know, was it grain
or the grate burning wood fell thru, the catas-
   trophe we knew could come at last come.
                                             We
   winged it as we could, watched our votes
float away, paper hats blown off to sea…
   Nub whose we would not be ours arrayed it-
self, say what we would against it no matter,

                                        say
   what we did, it adored itself. Mr. Hot Pot's
      heavenly glance atop his body had gotten
out of hand, Andreannette's body its antidote
   we thought but Andreannette's gloom lay like

                                             lead.
We knew no alchemy we knew, the way it lay,
   stood a chance, all the weight put on us pathe-
tic, the band we'd be, everyone's wanting the

                                        want-
   ing we'd pipe, some sub-equatorial squall's
humid poultice, exuviae caught in the wood we
   blew… "Sonance, be our boon," we piped.
                                             We
were Papuan Udhrite birds, whence we took
   the names of our beloveds. We were lovers
taking ourselves as precedent, hostages to

                                        qual-

ification though we were, sex-polis, apostol-
ic redoubt. Remembering the night I fell in love
   with Imas Permas, I piped loudly announcing

                                               my
      name was hers. Our weeping surroundings
   were the polis we brooded on, red-eyed sojour-
   ners that we were, secret cargo, immune to

                                             the
   enveloping
lash

                        •

   The scent of the beloved said to encumber
the tongue, the tongue's blue bewilderment
   song we'd been taught, the school of who

                                            when
      loving die. Love but only begun, we'd
   been taught, barely begun, the book of its
      bare beginning our book were there a book,
   the book of the would-be our book… Book

                                         meant
      more than calculable, the lovers' bare recum-
      bence naked beyond quantity, ordinance's fig-
   ures' forfeiture, ordinance's numbers' retreat.

                                            The
      beloved's bodily waft what respite impelled
   us, we the band we were, we the band we'd be,
      everyone's wanting our wanting. Naked recum-
   bence all we knew, naked recumbence all side

                                            and
      sly pondering, the slide of what would but be…
      The scent of the beloved said to waylay the
   tongue, talk though we would in some erstwhile

                                                  man-
      ner, the reed's lament never not audible, listen
      to the reed as we would. The reed wrote a letter
   we heard. What we'd hear was the letter the reed
      wrote, the scent of the reed's opening the scent of

                                                 the
      beloved, burnt opening intimate with lip, spit, eye
   tooth, burnt, odorous opening blown across. The

reed's burnt opening smelled of breath we heard

or

would hear, spit soaked into it we'd smell we heard
  or would hear, reed of the beloved's departure,

reed

 of the beloved's
kiss

•

We stood wondering what explained the comb-
  over. What was love, what was meaning, what
was breath, we were asking, now that Nub had

made

up its mind. We were the lovers we not yet were,
  the lovers we serenaded. We would not soon be
  done with them we knew nor would their like

soon

come again... *"We the pipers rub Nub the wrong*
  way," we announced, "we who went to school
at Djamil's knee. Love's low eminences, we among

the

  rushes, recumbence all we know, we of the Udh-
rite school." Letter less than edict, so read our reeds'
  decree. We drank beer brewed with polar ice melt,

we

  the dead who died of love's inconsequence. Wave
were it particular, water had it been thirst, Nub whose
  bread would be the bread of sorrow someday, Nub
so without soul we staggered back. A prepared place it

was

  loomed on high, an Osirian recumbency we were in...
  Angered by the comb-over's rise, we stood wonder-
ing, recumbency not as yet sex-polis, sex-polis not as yet

hope's

  remand. All it was was a flap of hair hiding something,
  all it was was tit for tat. We played on as we always
had. My new name Imas burred my intonation, a don't-let-
me-break-down sound I took toward bliss, the reed a bit

whose

horse I was. The reed's letter was its parlay-cheval-ou, the
  reed's complaint its tell-my-horse, the reed I bit down

on and blew, the reed we all bit on and blew, overghost as
we
    always had… I remembered the night I fell in love with
Imas again, a reed among the rushes, one among many,
the band in which each was all as well as one, each with
our
    sweetest remembrance gone bittersweet, an anxious taste
on our tongues. We were marching now. I lugged my
bad leg, its hitch gave us ythm, deep ourkestral heave and
misgiving. Legba strode with us we knew. Imas's voice
flut-
    tered like a candle flame caught in a draft, what world
was left a ball of dirt we strode across… As Majnoun
had lain eyes on Leila, my ears heard Imas's voice, a
hoo-
    poe with clipped wings it seemed. The night I fell she
took me to Java, another Java music made of the one
where she lived. The way she sang had a straining way to
it.
    We buttered our bread with suspect butter, ate raw meat
we were told had been cooked, lied to about the simplest
things. There was a gunmetal taste on our tongues, a feeling
for
    bullets and what was to come… Oyo Suwardi's reed
worried mine, the suling's lament unignorable, the suling's
weeping-daughter complaint. We were in the Moving
Star Hall, unbeknownst. We were in the Moving Star Hall,
dis-
    posable earth at our feet. We were in the Moving Star Hall,
overghost… Even so, I fell. Even so, fell hard. It was
the night I fell all over again. Even so, I was alright with it,
al-
    right with not being alright, beginning to leave myself, as
we all were, apart from ourselves, overghost. What would
Nub's next move be we wondered, caroling light, light not
oth-
    erwise to be had… Light not otherwise to be heard, we
piped on, live in the Field of Reeds, live on the Plain of
Quill, a feathered sprawl's excursion, gravelly word coax-
ing gravelly word. A lipless face suddenly loomed, moonlike,
sang
    with its eyes it seemed. We buttered our bread with suspect
butter again, laughed at the infernal comedy it was, we

let the reeds have their say. They wanted to say the world was
  wrong, the world we built the world built on our backs, and
                                                          they
said it, wanted to say it might be made right... It was that part
  caught them up, caught them out, hope with its hand out
  again. Overghost all of us, more than we could say, side-eye
                                                          and

  shade's do-
main

The scent of the beloved said to encumber
the tongue, the tongue's blue bewilderment
  song we'd been taught, the school of who

                                    when
      loving die. Love but only begun, we'd
been taught, barely begun, the book of its
  bare beginning our book were there a book,
the book of the would-be our book... Book

                                    meant
  more than calculable, the lovers' bare recum-
    bency naked beyond quantity, ordinance's fig-
ures' forfeiture, ordinance's numbers' retreat.
                                    The
    beloved's bodily waft what respite impelled
us, we the band we were, we the band we'd be,

                                    every-
      one's wanting our want-
ing

Nostrils wide with the scent of the beloved,
Mr. Hot Pot beheld Andreannette's approach. His
eyes lit on the ground in front of her, her

                                            feet,

    her ankletted ankles, her calves. All-out
wonder between her knees and waist as his
   eyes moved upward, love's own suzerainty it
seemed... Bodies were parts of bodies, parts

                                         of

    bodies the realm again. He remembered the
     feel of her sphincter tensing around his finger,
she the same, his tightening around hers, love's

                                    empy-

    rean body's bodily
fate

Still, they fed us fish with hard potatoes,
 shrimp so tiny they were brown we were
told. We scattered, crawling out and away.
                                        It
   was Nub wanting its face back, no other
way could we read it, up to any torment,
   fit sonance permitting… Some same story
                                      was
   on again, played out again and again…
   Tell-my-voice took issue with tell-my-horse…
   "Look at what time does," we were saying,
                                        sad,
      looking down at our-
   selves

BROTHER B'S RUMPSTRUCK RECITAL

—"mu" one hundred ninety-fourth part—

Barred at the gate where the music went,
no time soon would he be done with it he
  knew but went on pretending, what would

                                    nev-
    er, he was loath to admit, be made right,
  marred copy of what was true. We scratched
  our heads looking at him scratching his,
sat making what of it we could. Was it over

                                    now,
    we asked him, could he let go, let it go, be
done with it, move on. He said he'd long since
  cut it loose but no way, we knew, could that

                                    be
so… The tumbling out of it the it of it, the it
  of it going on. Was it love or the love song he
cut loose but couldn't cut loose we wondered,

                                    an-
    other Anuncio in love with the sound or the
  song of it, barred entry but entranced. We wanted
    to know was it a state he would give it up for, some
just and adjoined array of others wanting voice, the

                                    we
    our cresting récit mused and made mention of,
    the we he'd make real we hoped… Crepuscule
and candomblé wrought the we we sorted, what
    would not, least of all, turn out to've been govern-
  able, his to have exacted, his to have inspired, all

                                    our
  bumped imbroglio made worthwhile. Brother B
    had been speaking to that effect. Telephone poles
  whizzed by the dining car window as he let out a

                                    cry,
    convinced it would all be ours now, caught up in
  the cry and the calculi behind it, the new next aim
    our train sped toward. It was now, we knew, a train

                                    we
were on… This was in the distant past and only a mi-
  nute ago. He sat holding forth in the dining car as

we sat holding forth, the car a car the train long since
                                                    no
    longer had. So what were we we wanted to know
and where and how so, the he we projected having
    something of an answer, his the we we badly wanted
back. We were nothing if not of the moment, alive to
                                                    it
    declaring itself. Brother B was Mr. Hot Pot now. He
    wrote as though he wrote the reed's letter. No mention
made of his own low member, no mentioning the stiff
                                                    bou-
    quet emanating from it, he wrote in praise of Andrean-
nette's nether lips. He wrote extolling her low beard's
    accelerant musk, all of it a dream of some kind he awoke
                                                    from
    sweating, nakedness newly doomed he thought… He
was truly Mr. Hot Pot now. He wrote as though he wrote
    the reed's letter, his dream a dream of Andreannette's
                                                    jel-
ly. It was, he wrote, the world's one respite, the world
    old and mean, set in its ways. All this on a train that
had been a bus that had been a car that had been a house,
                                                    a
rant and a holding forth it was all we could do not to
                                                    rat-
ify

"I said some things it felt like life had wrung out
   of me," Brother B announced, back to himself,
back to being someone we knew or we thought
                                              we
   knew, at home with him and him at home with
us. Founding a new religion wasn't what he in-
   tended, sound as though it was though he did. A
                                         First
      Church of Jelly it might've been had he been
      intending it, a new and old gospel of Andrean-
         nette's perfume, waft he'd lain waylaid by... It
                                              was
   all an immaculate odor, no scent but the sound
      of it, a run he went off on, what always and anon
would lie underneath. "Up from under," he whis-
   pered, "I need bottom," something else life wrung
                                              out
      of him we took it, the train approaching a tunnel,
      the train going into the tunnel, the train coming out of
                                              the

      other
   side

Something seen in a face we'd long been
   chorusing. Something seen in Andreannette's
behind he now held forth about, of late come

                                                    to
   ask was that all it was... "Tail," he not so
much announced as expelled, spat as he ex-
   tolled it, Udhrite mince and remit. It was on-
ly a word, a word he threw down, only as if to

                                                    say,
   "Deal with it"... A rumpstruck recital was
   what it was, all it was. At odds with himself
we'd have said of him, himself caught in his

                                                    wan-
   dering eye, caught looking, wondering where
                                                    else
   it might
rest

We sought refuge, decapitism at us wher-
　　ever we looked. They were starting the next
　war, they were stealing the sky's ozone, it
　　　　　　　　　　　　　must-
　　　've been we were in Rum. It must've been
　we were in Mur, more and more talk of a
　wall going up, more and more moving back-
wards, Crater more and more dug in… Sister
　　　　　　　　　　　C

looked in of a sudden. She wanted to know
　　what was on the box. We lived on a bub-
ble of sound, not to be messed with. The box,
　　　　　　　　　　　we
　　said, had gone out to sea. The box had been
ours we thought but wasn't, this or that intuitive
　book our box we thought, sweet reason itself
　　　　　　　　　　　we
　　thought… Crater was calling itself Cradle,
　words now words' collapse. We were all the
　　more the Udhrite phalanx we'd be. To speak
　　　　　　　　　　as
with a new tongue we were seeking, tongue tip
　to tongue tip, tongues up on each other, the
　new tongue a double tongue it seemed. That the
　　　　　　　　　　　word
　　be on itself and be one with itself, tongue met
　demanding tongue. A slow, lingering kiss was all
　we had could we have been said to have that,
spoken for already, inimical words put on our lips,
　　　　　　　　　　　all
　　with, at the end, "what I'm talking about"… A
　　fickle sonance announced as much could we
　have heard it, a leak or a trickle of sound from
　far away, Neptune some would say, some would
　　　　　　　　　　　say
Jupiter… Space was our claim to kinship… Static
　　mussed our radio… Compensative light lit our
　　　　　　　　　　　way

　　that was no
　way

•

(trill)

I dreamed we lay savoring the small mercy love
   was, Andreannette and I down to it at last. It
was a dream we all had, Sister C and the women
                                    in-

cluded, a dream not having to do with whose
body had or didn't have what. Andreannette might
   have been André, Andreannette might've been
                                    An-

nette. Andreannette might've been Ornette,
Andreannette might have been Andrea… We lay
   in flight from whose body had what, sex-polis
                                 ta-

ken over by haystack and wind, straw in every-
   one's hair, straw on everyone's clothes. We
   were on this or that electrical contrivance. They
                                   were

saying something about an erectile college. Slav-
ery lived on some said… A closer look took us deep
into Nur, backwardswalking Nub's new low, new
limbo, our reaction to which again was to run. We lay
                                run-

ning, rabbits come after with shotguns and boots. We
   lay regaled, sprawl's rendezvous with sprint our
restitution, she of the rumpled pea coat, me of the let-
terman's jacket, dream silliness, ruse, regret… All
                                bets,

it wanted to say, were off, armor the way of the
world we were in, the two of us in bed fully dressed.
We lay still, moving thru the world at our leisure,
                                run's

quintessence abstract it seemed. A music made
of squiggles massaged us, the-box-not-having-left
   was back. We lay in our clothes knowing what lay
                                un-

derneath, who had what no concern. Grab was now the
   name we knew Nur by, not no matter we lay with-
   out hands having none of it but its foil, hands dipped
                                in

freezing water, ritual ablution we abjured it with…
We lay unhanded, we lay in flight from Grab and
Grope, Nur's twin principalities. "We lie choked in

                  our

tuxedoes," I blurted out, unclear why, unclear what
it meant. "We lie choked in our tuxedoes," Andrean-
nette blurted out in turn. Why were we in this place,

                  we

wondered, prone to say who knew what, tongues' au-
tonomy law. "We lie choked in our tuxedoes," we
repeated again and again… We were in the palace of

                  the

pea coat, housed under Andreannette's ex's drab
cover. Their two cats were in the sun room basking, a
domestic scene long since exploded she clung to,
all of it come to nothing, all as if it never happened, all

                  of

it wracked and repeating nothing ever was. "Leave it
all to them, this ball of dirt," we were now saying,
"the Nurians, give them their fill"… We imagined a we

                  be-

yond all calculation, the billowing pea coat a tent we
congregated under, reckoning love's more-than-one.
We opted out, no matter in's illusory offer, the it of it

                  ex-

punged, an it outside its proffer possible we thought, an
it whose it we lay in whose umbra. "Give it a don't-care
damn," we were saying now, "kiss it away," knowing

                  why,

knowing what we meant… We opted out, no get, no
grapple. We were knowing it would be alright, not being

                  al-

right would be
alright

Camarón sat us down as we wondered what
   next. That the box floated away told our des-
pair, hearts broken by politics again. Nub's
                                                face-
   lift had fallen, Nub's facelift had never
   been. We heard a hammering in our heads
and we wanted to hear more. We were post-
   post-something it said, it wasn't clear what the
                                                some-
   thing was... Comb-over was all scrape, scratch,
claw, post-face itself, pure post-. Bits of straw stuck
to our hair were bits of sound. We leaned on this
                                                or
   that eked-out sonance, the surge of one or an-
other more than we could hope for, mercy's wards
   again, mendicants again. Camarón's voice was
all strafe, a stray corona, sunspots pocking the air it
                                                car-
   ried, came
thru

_____

How could it have happened we milled around
gasping. How could hair look so much like hay
  we were asking, how could white be such a bright

                                                    or-
    ange... We trudged up a foothill, workers leav-
ing work, voices caught in the ground audible
  again, attenuated wide-mouth sound roofed in

                                                  stat-
    ic, sonority domed in static, hollow inside. How
    could the options they were calling history be so
  dread we were asking, the it of it against its ythm

                                                    no
      contest, the myth of it the real of choice... We
  trudged up a field of dry brush, our stomachs taken

                                                    out

        it felt
  like

SONG OF THE ANDOUMBOULOU: 217

—the eighth and ninth book of so—

The true annals of our would-be we continued
   unfolding, tonal forage paralleling life on plan-
et Nub. Everything not being alright would be

                                        al-
   right we'd left off knowing, gnostic remit we
so opted for. So said *The Book of So*, we couldn't
stop reading it, *The Book of So* said as much...

                                        We
   were deep into its back pages, we looked our-
   selves up, the we we were on our way to. *So*
   had been so leaned on, only to be leaned on a-
gain, consequent *so*, temporizing *so*, moot *so*,

                                       in-
   tensifying *so*... So said its tissue-thin leaves.
   So said its tree-trunk spine, revenant wood, a
caroling, chorusing book, stops out, up from un-
der, a boat from over the sea so what it was. Some

                                      said
   of it, "immune to what had been magic, amphi-
bian we thought," a book above water, a box below
   we guessed, new to such arcana, beginners again

                                       we
   felt... Morning met us twelve years behind our-
   selves. L.A. it now was we were in, Al Jarreau
what time it was, "Midnight Sun" so on the box

                                       we
   stood breathless, a cartouche encasing it all it
seemed. There had been getting to be too much to
and fro, too much getting farther away. Having

                                       put
   away qualm, having put away disquiet, peace
be upon us we begged, beset by mystical wishes, a
   fragility such that peace would not come. *Where*

                                       the
dead had gone had gone our need to be there, where
   the dead had gone had gone our need to know went
   the book's refrain, the book that would be caroling,

                                       the

book that would be a box... We sang with words
put in our mouths, a hoarse warbling, bird accom-
paniment, it might've been Baltimore we were in.

                                                    It

    might've been Upper Egypt we were in, Sheikh
Barrayn inside the book that would be a box. We
    were chanting the names of saints before we knew

                                            it,

    feathers caught in our throats, chanting the names
of places we'd been, Santa Barbara, San Diego, San
Jose. "We stake our lives on drunken bets all the time,"
the Sheikh had been saying before we broke into song,

                                                a

    bent all else accrues to he went on to expound as
    we sang... A song of the Andoumboulou it was we
sang, a two-in-one book of so, box and book's meet-
    ing, body and soul. Not since body met soul, we went

                                                to

say, semising, semisay, so of a mind as we were had we
    been. Night met us farther on, bird accompaniment
flown from our throats long since, word worn away by

                                            war-

    ble, warble pressed flat against the backs of our teeth,
    the song's unsettlement gone. Book nine it now was
    and had been all along unbeknown to us, our late syn-
tactic study a kind of swing. Not since body and soul's

                                            first

    meeting had road so run as one with song, song with
road... There was the sense that what we did was all copla,
    all ghazal, always in the air, always there to be plucked,

                                                pie-

    ces whose whole
we were

                    •

    So much had been said about *The Book of So*, so
    shaky a hold we had on it could we be said to've
had hold of it. No time soon would it be still, not

                                            be

    the jittery book it'd been, no matter we forever
said soon come. We tossed in our sleep lost in
    its pages. Dreaming's defeat we kept dreaming.

                                            A

strained happiness we read about stalked and
stayed with us, apocalypse taking aim as we dreamt
and kept dreaming, catastrophe whichever way

                                          we

looked... The book was in the house even so, a
stalked, stomped going forth with knees high, vio-
lin chirp taken up, high stepping. The book, some

                                        said,

was what was made of it, a weave and a waver-
ing the book itself said, all preface or prolegom-
enon should we finish, all afterword should we not.
The house itself, it was said, stepped high, bound by

                                        the

book inside it, the book about which talk never end-
ed, *so*'s having been said an advance on more say,
bound-to-be-said the house we sought out, a boast or a

                                        bri-

gade or both... So much had been said, so much
had been believed or disproved, it fell to us to reflect
on *binding*, a word we now took note of, a word

                                        we

for days turned over. It was *The Book of So*'s busi-
ness to be come back to, bound as it was and as we
as well were, carolers of dispatch though we were.

                                        A

treatise on bondage it turned for a time to be, an-
other stolen election under Nub's belt, the United
Slave States of Nub its name now, nothing if not all
that glittered, nothing if not a whistling bird. Canary

                                        yel-

low was thus the color we chose, Nub's new nature
its old and new nature, coal dust blackening our
tongues and our throats, a new kind of duende Nub's

                                        own...

We were living such that *so* summed everything
up, wished-for, would-be consequence inconsequent,
Nub's pendular politics back and forth... A Cape

                                        Ver-

dean piano hammered out glee we were shadowed
by, strained happiness we'd read about earlier come
true, only to be had at an angle, music's umpteenth

                                        re-

move

(19.xii.16: insofar-i)

An interrogative *so* caught me lost in the mo-
   ment, a million different ways not there. I kept
arriving by different routes, going nowhere, the

                                      same
   where again and again. "Like so," I said, com-
mending myself, a backhand slap, *so*'s minion,
  so's domain I so wound up in… It was the way

                                         it
   was in *The Book of So*, reading run by a wish
to get out, no way out the way it was in *The Book
of So*. I was the steal-away part, either a book
mark fallen to the floor or a drafted page put away

                                     and
   forgotten, given flow by such disposal, pure dis-
   patch… The Cape Verdean piano kept at me
no matter. Jorge Humberto was on the box or in

                                   the
book or even both, clubfoot happiness, halt felicity's

                                     fledg-

  ling
run

(20.xii.16: tag)

It got to where we were obsessed with *The*
  Book of So, so hung up we thought only of
it. We wanted to be gone or for it to be gone.
                                          We
     were living the dream, we were living the
  life. Part plaint, part plea, the Cape Verdean pi-
     ano was at our backs, an aspect of gallop
threaded in we heard as orishas, an aspect that

                                          would
  once have been all clack… Spirit ran thru it
     now, none of us anyone in particular it so took
  us out, none of us not in the spirit running thru.
                                          We
     were wanting to be the real we, we self-medi-
  cated, wanting to be the realest we… We wanted the
     book to involve us free of entrapment, we wanted

                                          to
  write the book more than
read it

(21.xii.16: tag)

   Everywhere we went everyone talked
about *The Book of So*, would-be we not
  to be caught out, would-be and real, we
                                were
   admonished, were in the same book…
We went to school underwater was what
  it was. Hoofbeats hollowed our bones and
                            we
  flew. A drunken run to the sea was what it
   was. A submerged run it turned out to be,
hoofbeats underwater exactly where the votes
                            went,
  hoofbeats under the
sea

THE TENTH AND THE ELEVENTH BOOK OF SO

—"mu" one hundred ninety-seventh part—

That was her once Mrs. P said, gazing
at a photo of herself, lost wondering again
   what time was. The bane and the boon
                              thought
   was it seemed at first, thought outside
thought she wanted to say. She instead
   said a staggered accretion we would do
                              well
to dismiss, a big bootheel blocking the sun...
   All this without speaking, said only to
herself or to thought itself. Meditative grace
                              the
   good feel it got, a hand addressing the cleft
of her ass could not have been closer, an in-
   side, simulant thing, a certain synonymy, an
                              all
   but exact symmetry, a saving asymmetry
it was. Mrs. P's ruminative gambit could be
   read and was read by Amadou's ghost it turned
out, Mr. P's amanuensis it turned out, so snug
                              they
were... The morning's horn had woken them
   both, the horn player's hand shaking it seemed,
horn less real than remembered. An eked-out
                              whin-
ny, a perspicacious neigh, the morning's horn
rode them, horse itself, like horses, a sound atop it-
   self they awoke having dreamt, they the horn's
                              is-
   sue they dreamt. The photo that was her once
lay on the nightstand. She leaned over, she looked
   at it closer, the she and the her she once was
not the same, the her not the she she was... Mr. P
                              said
   beware, thought's nemesis, hummed inside his
   Amadou head, barely there, loosely the he he'd
been, barely beside her, loosely the he he now was.
   Awkwardly it lay between them, stood between
                              them

once they were up, the thing that was Amadou's
ghost in its redactedness, the him-not-being-he
　　they lay in whose colors, a bullet-splattered drop
　　　　　　　　　　　　　　　　　　　　sheet
the floor their feet lit on… They awoke as from a
　　dream to another dream, the divine cartoon it was,
demiurgic joke at their expense, the words on their
　　　　　　　　　　　　　　　　　　　　　lips
not words but letters, Nub's new acronym U.S.S.N.,
　　　　　　　　　　　　　　　　　　　　　the

　　we they could no
way be

•

Citizens of who could say what splay na-
tion, Mr. and Mrs. P avidly availed of
one another, thrust and caress where their

                                          legs
met, sweet grab, sweet getting hold. They
  were what they called getting it on, ro-
  mance in the dark revisited, sweet adhesion

                                       the
  night before. Strained relation what it was,
touch their one certainty, with all but no words
or with none they spoke of exit, eros elegiac

                                   now…
No curve or declivity not marked, time took
  aim they knew. With all but no words or
with none but with lingam and yoni, avidly they

                                 a-
  vailed of each other, no caress not marked,
dark as it was and would be. Amadou's homego-
  ing never not with them, the Bahamian re-
minder on the box not more than a day ago, all

                                 re-
course while their bodies were intact only this
  recourse, the poverty of politics proven again,
  they caressed while they could because they

                               could,
kissed insistently, had they put it in words, "be-
fore the bullets come." So it was told in *The*
Book of So, so much more to it than could be told,

                               so's

  incumben-
  cy

We too heard the morning's horn, played
  so heavy by whoever played it, played hurt
by whoever it was played it, horn so heavy
                                          we
  the witnessing ones yelled out, "Don't drop
it!" We too heard it, shot body so taken to heart
  all there was left was wind and wailing, Mr.
                                      and
  Mrs. P having found what the rest left aban-
  doned in the dark, strained relation what re-
  lation there was… "A razor's edge what sang,"
                                      we
  said to each other, said to one another, bleeding,
                                      one
  to another, passing
  it on

•

The Book of So now itself more than ever,
   skin, bone, wrinkle, hair, dimple never more
the amenities they were, scar, blemish, bump

                                        nev-
   er more, they touched as though they sort-
ed out wounds, "Triage" the chapter they were
   in. They moved on to the eleventh book of

                                        so
sooner than they knew, the morning's horn's
   long throat scratchy, a severe sound out of
it even so... A Fanonian perplexity Mrs. P said

                                        it
   seemed, said not so much as thought, said to
herself. Mr. P, sensing her thought, called it
   bewilderment, a Fanonian bewilderment he

                                        said.
   They lay attending the wounded who were
themselves and the wounded inside themselves,
   the wounded ones the wise ones they'd been

                                        taught,
   they sought comfort in that... Not since Anuncio
   lay busted up had we the witnessing ones had
our hearts tugged at so, *The Book of So*'s way with

                                        it
   never more evident, we too lay wounded as
we read. The word *triage* popped into their heads
   whenever a word popped into their heads, the

                                        name-
sake chapter we lay in they lay in as well. So
   it went we wanted to say but shushed ourselves,
   loath to be caught looking in, witnessing we no

                                        mat-
   ter, the chorusing we we'd be still to come.
We were the we of cords and rattles and of call
   and response, edge enough to cut but a flat
surface now, a leaning we reflections fell off of,

                                        so's
new compendium a nether book they thumbed...
   "Please, Mr. and Mrs. P," we let out at last, okay

with being heard and wanting to be heard, caught

                                                   in

  the walls of the room they were in, the we whose

                                                       what-

say we were could walls
talk

•

Mr. and Mrs. Please they might've been, so
attendant to one another's pleasure, up for what
respite there was. A comely ponderousness

                                 about
her drew him in. "The perplexity of the liv-
ing" something said to've been said, Mr. and
Mrs. Perplexed they might've been… Bodies

                                 held
on to for life, hands rummaging one another's
orifices and crevices, a feel for protuberance
and fold let be at large, an appetite for curve and

                                 grain
let roam. The morning's horn blew gauge we
dreamt, we the witnessing walls, lifting ourselves.
"So it went" came out anyway, formulaic sense

                                 of
an ending, splay nation's beautifully bent intona-
tion wedding rhyme with exhaustion, torn up
tearing it up, worn out… "Love, if you love me"

                                 or
something like that, "If into love the image bur-
dens" or something, his and her ponderous come-
liness not to be hurried, his and hers yet to be had.

                                 A
glancing address, bent inclination, the way it was
they had without having or holding, knowing they
had having or holding enough, this the sense the

                                 horn
woke them with, a chatterbox piano behind it
when the box, the clock radio, went off… Mr. and
Mrs. P delved up to their eyes in one another's

                                 book,
ten turning into eleven repeatedly, each time the first

                                      time
again

Interrogative *so* had to do with consequence.
We wondered, as they did, what next. Interro-
gative *so* had to do with what to make of what
                                              just
    was. We wondered, as they did, what the hell.
    We were in the book, the book inside us, we swal-
    lowed it. We swallowed ourselves outside in,
so's notice's echo, squibs of sound caught in our
                                              hair
    like paint... A glossary would've helped, what to
      make of "gauge," "Fanonian," "chatterbox piano"
and such, such the way of going in *The Book of So* that
                                              there
      wasn't
one

•

The Book of So was the book our showing up
   wrote. What does it mean to say *so* it at once
   inquired, all or nothing the answer it angled
                                   for.
    We had fallen asleep counting ballots the
  night before, the night before taking off to
  Diddie Wa or to Wa Diddie it turned out,
                                mov-
  ing on occurring to us only then. "Like so,"
   it said before we could answer. *The Book of*
So had gone underground it seemed. No one
                             want-
   ed to know about *so* it insinuated… *The Book*
of So was as well the book our disappearing wrote,
  the answer all or nothing we were to've given,
                                we
   who wanted to hear about *so* no longer want-
  ed, *so* meaning consequence, what accrues. No
   longer wanted had we ever been wanted, we
were the wind in the walls or the walls themselves,
                             wind-
   ed. Breath bade us goodbye so quick we led wan-
   nabe lives, grubbed for whatever scraps came
our way… Vicarious legs were the legs we stood
                             on,
   walked on, ran on, someone else's legs we gazed
   out at, voices in the walls when someone thought
they heard voices, *The Book of So* close to the body
  and to the bone, chirping epiphany no end… Thus it
                             was
  we looked out at Mr. and Mrs. P, each the other's
mundane angel. Thus-it-was was in the air, thus-it-was
  was what we thought, thus-it-was was so-it-was's
                             dis-
  guise… Were we the walled-up spirit of conse-
  quence we wondered, something only *The Book of*
                           So
  could
say

Awoke from a dream to the waking dream,
   fold of another sort, other sorts... Paper
airplanes that had been ballots flew outside
                                    their
      window... Paper boats that had been bal-
   lots floated on the river that flowed to the
   sea... Paper hats that had been ballots sat on
                                    eve-
   ry head passing by out-
   side

Djed stood bereft among the crew we'd be-
come, Djed from whom, no matter he rode
  with us, we hadn't heard in ages. He grew
                              tired,
   he said, of smartass effects. What to say,
  what to say was again the question. What-
  ever tapping the heels of our hands together
meant, he said, was what. We the walled-in
                         cho-
  rus commented on what went on, nakedness
  no longer new to us but strained, edging
on soul, having to do with soul we'd heard it
                        said...
   Consequence's ambassadors, we sang a sus-
  pect serenade, the spirits or the ushers or the
  ghosts of sequentiality, everything scattered
                     now.
History the poverty of time, Djed insisted, one
  throw among possible throws, otherwise extra-
  vagant, why was oil behind it all, why bill, why
                  bul-
  let. He was beginning to tear his hair as he
spoke, the rest of us as well, bald before long, in-
  side the walls enclosing the room asking why
wall, why repellent, why not the wind we were, the
                  else-
  where no matter where, the nowhere ever kept
  out... What and wherefore's metaphysical decree
it was he advanced, Djed for whom all else fell in-
  to inconsequence, capitulation to spirit, as he put it,
                  what
  bore weight or nothing would, metaphysical wont
few but we, he propounded, knew. Anuncio at once
  piped up, wanting none of it, the we thus exhorted a
                  cho-
sen few he said he had no use for, no way would he
  agree. Walled-up in mind alone, we were sprung
by Anuncio's objection, out into the room and outside
                  the
  room, Mr. and Mrs. P's reconnoiter. It was Brown

versus Bardo for the millionth time, them all in our minds,
us all in theirs, Mr. and Mrs. P's outlier boudoir. What

                                                   to

    say, what to say Djed asked again even so. What-
ever tapping the heels of our hands together meant, he
   said again, was what, the willingness of spirit what,

                                            A-

nuncio's objection no mat-
ter

●

We felt better being out, far from Lone
   Coast though we were, far from Low For-
  est. Spirit's behest his lone concern Djed
                      kept
  repeating. Sheer metaphysical conceit A-
   nuncio said. A canary egged Anuncio
on Sophia said, suggested we were miners un-
  derground the way she said it, black lung
                    Nub's
  new G.D.P. She said Djed stood in wor-
shipful regard of what lay under, looking up at
  what lay under the riffling of spirit thru his
                  be-
  loved's dress, no different from Anuncio
in that regard she said, both laboring under apt
  illusion... The rest of us turned away from their
talk. We'd heard it all before. An Algerian banjo
                  on
  the box we knew right away was Dahmane El
   Harrachi got hold of us, phlegm forever caught
in his throat that might have been coal dust, an
                  ob-
structed sound pulling us in. What to say, what
  to say he might have been singing, hitch and flu-
  idity so united can't-say and say were the same...
                  We
  were at the point on our trip where counter-say
and say rode with us, members of our crew as much
  as any of us, Counter-Say and Say in *The Book*
                  of
  So. Djed feared himself a slot dictated by the
book, Anuncio too, canary tweet wound with
  banjo cluck, an acoustical contagion they drew
                  out,
  drew on. All in the fullness of what was to come
  Sophia said, hers the exegetical slot Anuncio's re-
butted, no such presumption he replied... We felt
                  like
  puppets, feared we were puppets, out from in-
side the walls but unfree, gotten to by canary chirp,
  chaabi, comb-over's rise, doorpeeps in the great

outdoors… Remembering the room and the wood
                                        the
   shelves and the paneling were made of, pine made
   us think of Low Forest, redwood made us think
of Lone Coast, what to say what tapping wood with
                                           our
   knuckles
meant

_____

(3.i.17: insofar-i)

I woke up worn out. Medicine made me
   sick. Djed's mystic remit was more mystic
than I could stomach, at odds with its long

                       odds

   on exit, I saw no way out. The wall made
me an erstwhile Mr. P, an uprooted reed to
   Mrs. P's earthical girth… I was weary, as if

                     their

   book forced my hand, the reed's low recon-
noiter's negation. At song's end I held my breath,
   Mrs. P making up for what Mr. P lacked, Mr.
P making up for what Mrs. P lacked, an equation

                   con-

   cocted in hell perhaps, the sum they amounted
   to cracked… So at least went the way of rhyme's

                rea-

   son, the squeeze doorpeep un-
packed

•

Each the other's mundane angel echoed,
buffeted from wall to wall, the walls we the wit-
    nessing ones were caught inside. Nothing if
                                        not

    angelicity's mandate, what love's undone
angels dictated, a house whose windowpanes
    were cinder blocks opened onto incoming
surf... It was a dream of Lone Coast a trillion
                                    miles

    from Lone Coast, an obscurely sonic sphere.
Each the other's undone angel echoed as
well, mundanity's way we thought it was. Our
    heads were heavy, hard to keep on, subject to a
                                    time-

    lapse bobble now and again, almost like a shi-
ver but orbital, a wagering of tilt against neck
    strength, a bending back to look up at the sky...
                                        Each

    the other angel's mandate also echoed, words
again too spindly a medium, rickety legs the house
    we were in stood on. *Each the other's echoed*
                                    man-

date reverberated long into the night, angelic reci-
    procity's day long done, Mr. and Mrs. P's récit.
A story told x times over, x's upper limit said to be
                                        num-

    berless, finitude's tale to itself... Djed's admoni-
tion stayed with us, Mr. and Mrs. P's would-be sexit
    notwithstanding, history the poverty of time. Time
not yet enough nor run out, always not enough nor run
                                            out.

    Whatever fund it was event came out of, whatever
        stash, whatever store, shades of what Djed had
said kept at us... To caress was to rub away polis, Mr.
                                            and

    Mrs. P lay bare but for us looking out at them, disa-
vow the wall though we did, walled in, doorpeep's
    epiphany there was no epiphany, they who'd have
                                        put

    history a-
way

The box had been helping them live another
　　life, the he whose predicate Mr. P was,
the she Mrs. P likewise. The same had been
　　　　　　　　　　　　　　　　　true
　　of the book. It gave them another chance,
other chances, a way they lived athwart them-
　　selves, throve on recension, an awayness
　　　　　　　　　　　　　　　　al-
　　ways keen to arrive… There were also
the rest of us looking on, habitués of the
　　almost, apprentices of a sort, doorpeep acad-
emy the school whose attendants we were,
　　　　　　　　　　　　　　　　come
　　to the planet clueless, what to say. What to
say, the heels of our hands together, what, eve-
　　ryone wincing, some outright crying, come
　　　　　　　　　　　　　　　　here
　　not knowing
　what

What was key was we ran parallel to our-
    selves, the willingness Djed spoke of
parallel to itself, the book what arose from
                                    that.
    We were tapping the heels of our hands
    together, they did as well. Neither group
        was mirror, wood, a mere replica of the oth-
er. We moved or stood as Duke would say,
                                    paral-
    lel to… What we wanted was to find our-
    selves flung, fetch bearing on us less than far,
        a sense we were more than where, more
                                    than
        once, Monk's monastic agreement, Monk's
                                    pla-
    tonic spat, one on one,
off one

SONG OF THE ANDOUMBOULOU: 219½

—insofarian rally, insofarian arrest—

I felt like I was back in the Bahamas. I
   was a lizard wearing a red bowtie. My
ears were burning, I was Mr. Whatsay,
                         my
   ears were candy-apple red. A crown
someone threw away hit me in the ribs,
   a trombone in the upper room groaned. I
                          de-
   cided until my ears went back to being
     brown I was done, I was trying not to let
polis take me out. I wished I could believe
                       like
   Huff pretended to. I wanted not to believe
he only pretended to believe. The people, he
   said, will win... I wanted to believe it, so
I said it too. The people, I said, will win. I felt
                       like
   I was back where I'd never been, I was Mr.
Whatsay. Day after day I spoke with Huff. Day
after day I asked him say what but I wasn't
                       the
   what-sayer. I was what the what-sayer said,
I was Mr. Whatsay, said to've been the Ps's
   walled-in appetite, Crater was in my stomach
                       it
felt like... I sought cosmic solace, none to be
   found. I wanted my East, bodily breakdown
                       the
 one certain launch there
was

MANY A MUSIC NOT EXACTLY SONG

—"mu" one hundred ninety-ninth part—

Once out of the wall we found ourselves at
   a loss. We were in Crater's pit again, way
past the Dread Lakes region, Dread Lakes

                      a

   relative walk in the park. We rolled rocks
up Crater's walls, rocks that were bales of
   cotton, Mississyphean rocks were bales that

                    rolled

    back down… Better had it been unendur-
  able, better what it built not been built we
    thought, better we'd been left alone, better
the world had been left alone. The crackling

                 of

   the record in the air made us weep, we of the
     bound ankles, horn blare inflected in a way
    that drew blood, music the cups it always

                was…

We stood sipping, we got our heads cloudy,
   quaff too deep to keep down it turned out,
a bitter book troubling our stomachs, our ears

              rang

    softly but rang. Most like music when same-
ness marked and permuted itself, our reputed
   rapport with death more shotgun wedding we

             said.

A lure for feeling, we'd read, as though feeling
   were to be caught, fish nibbling away at the book
that took us in, whatsay substantive we said it so

            much,

   a music not exactly song left us drunk, many
   a music not exactly song… The more it was mu-
sic the more astringent, an abstract dishevelment
   purveyed in blasé brogue, better to've been so bad

            no

   music availed us, hit by the nuke our passage a-
mounted to, work songs' mercy no mercy, so bad

          we

 vapor-
ized

•

Many a music not exactly song surveilled us,
   the thing happening we were calling time,
not knowing what. Many a midnight headsweat
                                        a-
   nointed us, no matter we slid in Crater, what-
ever begged off being what it was more what
   it was. Sonny's house of growl was back on the
                                        box,
   music wanting not to be music it sounded like.
No matter we slipped and we slid, music not want-
   ing to be music would be music it screamed, the
                                        great
   work of the *not* still to come... So that restraint
or constraint itself "sang," an ars poetica sort of
   in the air, an air of angularity not inversion. What-
ever begged off being what it was was become by
                                        re-
   luctance, whatever so begged being more what
   it was. In arrears a more obvious music, all we
could do was call our predicament names, Mississy-
   siphus the lone one we could think of, we felt so
                                        ta-
   ken, we felt so had... Insofar as we sang it was
again the same, some inevitable two feeling some-
   thing between them, not sure what beyond wounded-
ness the something, belly and loins' republic their
   country could they construe it. Insofar as we sang
                                        the
   sky was blue and the sun so bright we'd live forev-
   er, many a music not exactly song notwithstanding,
an attitude all we meant, a wariness not to be caught,
   light's recombinatory thread the dress we wore... The
                                        more
   light shredded the more armored we stood, many a
music not exactly prized an appurtenance, all of it so
   gone toward reaching without reaching, not since the
                                        qui-
   ver grown of po, the sirening fonio so known to it-
self. Nudge played many a music not exactly song,

nudge not exactly wanting but wanting, a warning it

                                                  let

   itself go
  with

•

As much as it felt like home it wasn't home.
Chronophobic Tête reeled in awareness time
went by. *Mundane angels though we were, we*
                                        spoke
    of love, love as it was told of in love lore, the
    love-region love's religion of yore. So began
    the marginalia she wrote in *The Book of So.* So
was what music not exactly song was. So was
                                        the
    bearing-down of all that obtained and of all
        that impended, a wall more three-dimension-
al than most… Squat purview she named it, ex-
iting slate upon slate. *Might a caress bring it*
                                        down,
        she wrote, a sigh folded into each word she
    wrote, *dreams a track of losses, Nub's teeth*
    naked again. As much as it felt like home it
                                        was-
    n't her insistence was, late transit from the prac-
        tice rooms of Eden, nothing if not kingdom come.
We stood on the sidelines appraising Utopia, bank-
rupt we'd long since been told… As much as it felt
                                        like
    home it wasn't home, song announcing itself null
    a music nonetheless, we were lingering among the
    syllables, sound a stout lozenge we let minister our
throats, a thing happening we were calling time, naming
                                        what
        we knew nothing about. Kaushiki's pipes took it to
    the sky off in the background, harmonium beneficence
    our ground and ongoingness, going's long abidance
                                        we'd
    see

Tête's run made her legs hurt, her body the
   body politic's infection it felt like, no getting
out, no getting away, no getting on. Who'd
                              have
   thought Tête would so step up we all thought,
many a bank with no river in sight quintes-
   sential Crater, the untogetherness of it gave
                              us
   pause. The untowardness it turned out, a
sense we'd all be taken out we dwelt on, well
   into comb-over country now... I stole away
the best I could. I was feeling the world a certain
                              way.
   Paul Gonsalves, Johnny Hartman popped up. The
way the brothers of my mother's generation must
                              have
   I thought

All we wanted was to be prophecy's would-be
   seal, a puzzlement to've taken pride in, an
emotive disarray or dismay, some way of coping,
                                              nev-
   er not the stuff of what spoke loudly, spoke
loudest, the gods again pathetic we felt it so deep-
   ly, something so unreachably broken we drew
                                              back
numb… We were out in free time now, hit so
   hard we could only speak sideways, no telling
                                              what
   would come up
next

A painting hung on the wall we'd been in-
    side we saw once we were out, white with
  its passionate pink a pale token, answered
                                        by
    ythmic brown's mere myth no matter, a
  deeper jointure there to be found… Less
    in love with love than the song of it some
                                        said,
  my head swam so much was going on. Many
    a music not exactly song took a toll, banks no
                                        riv-
    ers ran be-
  tween

SONG OF THE ANDOUMBOULOU: 220½

—the overghost ourkestra's nonsong—

Where did our votes go we overblew let-
   ting the reeds ask, hew to the real though
we would or would try, readying for war
                             as if
   war had ever left, again the closer walk
long sung about, thought about, verging
   nigh… Many a music not exactly song's im-
plied imminence, something song might've
                              been
   whose harbinger were there song, some-
thing we thought, thinking some farther brink
   song insisted on, song so assured it recused
                              it-
self… An invisible key turned each river that
   wasn't there, jihad and crusade's crossfire
we were caught in, the Nubsters up to their Nub-
ness again. When would we be free of it we
                           begged.
   We wanted not to be of the book in that way,
the so-called open-and-shut. There was a book
   we wanted not to be done with, *The So-Called*
Book of So some called it… We called it simply
                           The
   Book of So, wanting it drummed in so deep we
dreamt it real, the book we knew not otherwise was.
But as was, we were schooled in its pages, the true
                         one,
   truly one, as was
could be

ANUNCIO'S TWELFTH LAST LOVE SONG

—"mu" two hundredth part—

We sat with our backs against the head-
   board, arms around each other's waist, legs
out in front. My eye followed her left calf's
                       in-
   side curve, ran to some beyond it seemed
     it got at, the beauty both its own and that
   of what it angled toward, nothing or a
                       cer-
tain something not to be known. Lean for-
   ward, reach, touch and caress it though I
might, lean forward, reach, touch and caress
                       it
   though I did, nothing or a certain something
     kept capture at bay… Meanwhile, "Time,"
   the man belted out on the box, "has a story," a
                    son-
   ic republic espoused as we espoused anoth-
er. Arms around each other, hands all over each
   other, a tactile commonwealth we espoused.
The comb-over cloud darkened even that, so ab-
   ject we had to laugh or it made us laugh, the
                  ghost
   of Lorca shot by Franco's minions quizzical we
    laughed, laughing not to cry he came to see…
Audiotactility plied our abidance, the been-there we
                    knew
   loosely as so. "So's no book but it has a book," I
said. "Its lament is that the book arrives only after."
Anuncia shifted, pulled away, abruptly a birdlike
                  lady
   to my right. "Tell so be happy it arrives at all,"
she said, salty, a bee or at least a buzz up her bon-
   net it seemed. I suddenly wept, "It's all coming to
an end." "Not all," she consoled me, "only our part
                 of
it"… I felt myself lifted, the earth a peppercorn on
   my tongue… Bodily decline. Bodily divestiture…
                 The

creaking of the spirit come
nigh

            •

Among the instructions not so much as a whisper,
  the new instruction book on the bedside stand.
Sacrosanct, I concluded, not to be talked about, late
                        lore
  how not to unravel. It was getting to be such time
as that it seemed, a broken wishbone thought to've
  been a sundial, what time it was the shadow it cast...
The promise of hips abided, still stood, the draw they
                      were
  they'd always be. I told myself that, telling Anuncia so
as well, bodily allure the lone assurance I clung to
she chided me, so's book less reliable she'd allow. It'd
                  be
  the music we might've made, she went on, might we
    have made music, no matter many-a-music-not-exact-
    ly-song's gray augur... It was my last last love song
                 she
  meant to say, she went on to say, my concern with so's
lament harboring another... She was Anuncia the Numinous,
Anuncia the Not-Nonchalant, Anuncia, name or no name,
                       not

  to be messed
with

            •

I related the broadness of her back to the sky, a Euli-
pian air on the box moving on. "Box, go my bond," I
  begged it, the theft brought us there we pondered most.
                    What
    was gnostic about it, what was flam. What her broad
back's expanse drew salt from, dip trade the skin game's
  game, the was the where's contortion, the where lay
                  be-
tween... To sit that way put me in a state. Stars had been
  known to pace the backs of our heads, points joined like
                 hands,
  a time way back it happened all the
time

•

(book of so)

Lingering waft, intimate fold and recess a kind of
   commission, I stayed up late to look at her sleep-
  ing face. Some unavailable Anuncia I looked at
                                        or
   looked for, lost in looking, something-seen-in-a-
  face I'd seen before… *Lingering waft a kind of incu-*
  bus, "Waft, move my quill," I wrote. *An affront to*
                                   love
   Nub's calculable beneficence, not so much recur-
  sion as return, I wrote. Anger rode my thumb, Nub's
  new relinquishment Nur run amok, readiness gone
                                    off
  I saw. What was this or that proffered haunch given
   that I wondered, riled myself, unable to say, knew by
 nonsay it was a last love song I wrote, getting to be the
                                   lone
  love song I wrote, long on being done with it, of waft
 even saying I'd have none, I'd have no more of it, the
  one song I wrote sworn off… An onslaught of snow blew
                                  in
   outside, Nub's weather wintry again, Nub's collapse in-
  to Crater we held each other against when she awoke. A
  sweet scene it might've been looked at from outside. An
                                 emp-
 tying out of ourselves it felt more like, soul taken after by
  the scare that was about, fright so close to the bone we
                                let
 ourselves
 go

Dreams broke me down all night, similitude a mat-
  ter of touch. Eyes out or eyes out of it it seemed,
apt enough looking at all we were loath to hear talked

                                                    a-
    bout, we of the audiotactile way beyond it now... I
  touched her skin and fell back broken, brought out, more
  to answer for now than before. Less lean coming out

                                                    than
  going in, chance's gloss was chance's ghost... As if to
    say, "Wrack, be my wand, my raft, my witness," as if

                                                    to
    but not, standing
  pat

Had I been able to be done with waft and masque-
    rade, musk a mask I lifted, waft a cloud I cut
    thru... Had Nur's horn not stood as congealed as

                                                    a
        rhino's, pinpoint sharp at its tip. Had the snow
    not caught us unawares, mounting at the base of
        Jump Tower, white shredded-paper confetti, torn-
    up tickets, token vote... Could cover not've drawn

                                                  my
        eyes to what lay covered, waft its ulterior witness
                                                I'd be

        no more privy
        to

Not sure I was awake, I woke up asking
    was it Jump or was it Bump, not-knowing
  folded into the structure itself it seemed. A
                                            rent
      party in the penthouse it seemed, Jump
    Tower's blowout sale, Bump Tower's, to get
      the "stolen" trophy back another prophy-
  lactic war... We stood with Stesichorus. An
                                            il-
    lusion it all was, a spell black alchemy cast,
      as all that was to follow would be. Was it
  time's grudge against itself, we wondered, made
                                            it
      so messed up, a first moment no other could
  be we lamented, never another anything like the
    first. An answer, dark light, shone in the asking,
                                            a
      certain something outside all say, all other see,
    something seen only at a glance... No matter the
      cosmic solace we sought, the cosmos lay disconso-
  late, hostage to what none could be like. Waft was
                                            all
      there was at day's end or beginning, the lovers'
    dark, musty bouquet. Fraught harbinger, waft an
  apt adamance. Flush against it, eternity time's cap-
    tive, timeless moment merely a wish. The I no
                                            long-
      er mine but another's, we were now calling
    ourselves We-Who-Saw-It-Coming. "I lay with a
      ghost," Sophia bolted awake proclaiming. "We
                                            lay
  on a bed or a couch in London back in the day,"
    she went on. "In those days I called myself Zvia"...
  The ghost lay naked, a man modeling naked she
                                            paint-
    ed, testicles and penis prominent against his thigh,
  the way he lay there nonchalant. We all saw it, an
    idyllic tableau. That it ever happened, we could see,
                                            re-
      manded her, back the way it was, back to the old

name she took, ours now We-Who-Saw-It-All… "But
   fingers turn to dust as we touch," she said, "arms up

                                                    in

smoke as we embrace, come Jump or come Bump,
   lips rub away as we kiss…" "Don't let's go there,"

                                              we

   said

     Sophia donned an ambient cloud she called
Zvia, paint a gray somnolence, dream and
  dream-water at once. We lived her sadness,
                                        "Don't
  let's go there" no matter. She piped like a
long-note piper, a cimbalom's clang under-
  wrote it all. We hung our heads, bowed our
                                     heads,
  necks meditation-weary, our necks no longer
   with us, numb to the world and to us inside the
world, some cut we saw coming soon come… It
                                  was
  all a boxed waft one got off on she'd find a way
to say in paint, she said, box not the release waft
  proffered, boxed meant anything but. "Zvia," we
                                 pled,
  deadpan, "don't," but she went on. "Zvia," we
went on pleading. Our mouths filled up with he-
  lium, our voices went chipmunk high. "Zvia," we
pled, no longer deadpan, "don't," divine-comedic
                                 chirp,

  cartoon
clip

●

So was afoot someone cried out, consequence's
   awaited day at last come, Zvia's gray drapes
lately drawn, a lived elegy, no sun but a pathetic
                                                  uni-

   verse lit up. We perked our ears to what sough
had to say, sigh, susurration, its own the suzerainty
   brought us up short. Something I heard I thought
                                                  I'd

      heard before, I'd have sworn I'd heard before...
So was afoot, the pathetic universe astir, pain made
   for by corner after corner with nary a taco truck.
Zvia's palette, mostly blacks and grays, might have
                                                  been

   debris wood was after burning. We throve anyway
      on tonic travel, utterly dry, utterly drunk, none
of us knew which. Our sense was that they met some-
   where, exactly where we were, none of us able to
                                                  say

   exactly where... We throve on tonic travel, nervous
though we were. We throve on tonic travel even so,
   so so afoot, Jump turn out to be Bump grown to be to
                                                  our

      liking, Nub, Nur, Jump a bump in the road, road our
rescue again. We throve on tonic travel, sonic traipse,
   ready for what was to come, rasp in our throats a re-
minder, a letter short of grasp taunting us. "Don't let's"
                                                  pro-

   tected us it felt like, a coat of sheerest lacquer it sur-
      rounded us with, a bubble it involved us in... A chilly
wind blew thru cracks in the heartland, mud between
                                                  logs

   no matter. We could've been broken in on with guns
we knew but it would've taken that, God's left hand
   we had heard it called, guns God's favor, a sign. Past
                                                  an-

ger present, present anger, ill wind. A forked tongue
   said to've been spoken with, wind come off it again...
Anywhere but Nub's middle we pled not knowing we
                                                  pled,

   Zvia's paint's appeal, eyes dry, ears wet, unclear. Either
we were in Nub, Nur, Jump or we were in London. Lon-

don it turned out we were in, taken out, in, by tonic travel,

                                                    son-
ic traipse

Who'd have thought we'd have traded Lone Coast
for London we thought, as if Nub tying flame to our
   bodies wasn't enough. Black attitude abounded, black

                                                        or

   bleak or the gray semblance the sky redacted, Zvia's
lay ministry of paint as of charred wood, to've had a
   sense of having lived was what it was. Much talk of

                                                       the

end of the world and it was, beautiful ball of dirt soon
   gone. We were caroling day's late arrival, a grave note
to enter on. Jump Tower fell we'd been dreaming, blew

                                                     Lone

   Coast away... Not sure we were awake, we saw smoke
fold what ground there was away, a way, we thought, of
   lifting our feet without lifting our feet, a closer, too-close

                                                      walk

   we leaned into. I wanted night to be night again, no such
awakening as the one we were having, loose cheer not to go

                                                      off,

   hatchets hang in the
sky

We kept pleading, "Don't." We kept calling
her name. "Zvia" was a mantra now. We
kept entreating, "Please, Zvia, don't," but she

                                   went

  on. We lived her life in London, we wore the
gray paint she wore… We got away anyway
  from Jump, away from Bump, away from Nub's

                                   new

  confederacy. Another world it was her light car-
riage offered us, a horse-faced lady's birdlike body's

                                   re-

lay

II

RUN

SOPHIA'S BURNT-WOOD OPENING

—"mu" two hundred second part—

I walked on in or even walked on thru, Chuck
   Jackson on the box, Blood Ulmer right after,
  whose broken hearts it fell to me to mend.
                                As
    if no moment were stolen, sand before we
  knew it water, drought's drinkable ocean lapped
  off Lone Coast, late salt insistence no match
                                  for
my too-close walk... All I wanted was that, that
   was all I wanted, say-it-again's logic a wand
I walked on in with, Zvia's drapeless muse, had
                                   it
  to be someone, was me. I was or I wanted to be
   the implied but unstated accent, stress fall to me
as to one whose mood was legion, bruited-about
                                ac-
  claim Sophia's burnt-wood paint applied. I was
her lost Egyptian lover. I trod a mat that was the
  floor of a reed boat, would-be boat of the sun my
                                feet
  attested, would-be Osirian strut... I walked need-
 ing only two dimensions, flat, sideways it seemed,
  burnt wood an incense my nose flared letting in, the
sublimate scent was to ashes, the affine char was to
                              paint...
I walked on in, even walked on thru, Sophia's con-
  sort, Zvia's main squeeze, the end of all heartbreak,
                              bird-
 boned a-
gain

Were bone and body landlord to soul's tenant,
   the wealthy to the world, I wanted to know.
Ever on the move at the landlords' bidding, it
                                        was-
   n't touring but a kind of terror, tour though
we made of it no matter, tour that we made of it
all there was... My body a field of play and
                                        hers
too, the wonder of legs and what lay between.
   Our last legs we awoke knowing we now walked
on, as if grave dust was ours to do as we want
                                        with,
   the difference an "o" or an "e" made, the boon we
                                        took

   bone to
be

•

Something some were calling beauty put a stamp
  on doom, gilded splinter turned rickety limb.
  Zvia daubed an odd perfume on her breastbone,
                                             waft

  I faintly recollected, recalled we kissed with a
hint of almond on our tongues... Not since finger
  met fold body and soul such high silence, dark
                                             tele-
    pathy telepathic in the dark. Step, steady or not,
  loomed everywhere. I felt my bones float when-
    ever I moved my legs. Earth more avaricious year to
year, I went afraid I'd fall, the ground more prone to
                                             pull
    it felt like, legs eventually taken out from under...
    So that if I saw myself I saw myself knocked over,
the prey of what loomed indomitable, pink luxury
  though it bore, blood's blessing, Zvia's block body's
                                             gray
    foreboding. I wanted to see blood's presence darken
her skin. I wanted her face drawn orgasm-tight. I want-
ed her chest flat, breasts against her ribcage, I want-
ed her flat on her back like me. I wanted her light-bodied
                                             big-
    ness's float-away gospel, the thought of whose girth or
    the thought of that thought, the bounty being naked
  would be... Gray said put those thoughts away, put away
                                             dalli-
    ance. Nub's unpoliced anger, Nub's angry police, banged at
                                             our
    door

Gray culled it, called it, thick in-between bra-
vura all its own, consummate charcoal, boon bone's
   cousin it seemed. Burnt bamboo openings opened

                                                   or

   closed and one blown over, something like "sa-
cred" the word we'd have used for it, blown open,
   seeming to say life no longer lived… All as though

                                              we

   low-rode a fleet of rented Priuses, the melted-icecap
martinis once we got where we were going no matter.
   All as if we were conflicted gnostics it turned out, gray

                                              paint

saving the planet, gray paint's burning
wood

The sun was a fallen furnace caught in the trees'
   naked limbs, my sun boat burned to a crisp. Gilded
splinters had nothing on me I thought even so, life
                                      the
   long farewell it was no matter. "Say your little
piece and be done," something in my head said, "say
it now." More talk of say so made the mixed figure
I was and it was it seemed it took a page out of so's
                                    book...
   My gait faltered. I strode wobbly-legged, a fake sail-
or, seeming puppet of say and so, my boat no more than
                                      cin-

  ders now

Andreannette was our roadside Madon-
   na, her ex's peacoat no Shroud of Turin
but close, all was as it was but also not.
                                So
   said Zvia. The it of it of many names
of no one of them, *absconditus* caught
   in our throats had it ever occurred to us,
                             we
   put our roadside devotions away... It
was blue against gray again, Nub's confed-
   erate ghost once at our heels in our faces
                            now.
We were back in the war zone, newly know-
   ing we never left. It was a critique of ra-
tionale we were advancing, a critique of the
                         creak
   of mere reason, Nub's now whispering not-
say whistling Dixie, photos amid flowers, candles
   lit to the newly taken, one's head a roadside
                        cas-
ualty, roadside shrine... How to speak of what
   binged on speech, the conversation we were
said to be having all talk, say's whatsaid not-say.
                       How
   many centuries of say could more say do away
with, how much more say and how soon. Zvia
   asked all this, said all this, her gray said it, gray
paint we were stuck in, said we were the company
                       mis-
   ery keeps. We were writing a book on love gray
   said, a book of song said more than once to be on
a box, the box a recursive construct all manner of
                       say
   contrived, as though such being as not being on it
ever was... Our jaws pulled away from the sides of
   our faces, jawbone relinquishment a drift it seemed
                       lift-
   ed us. "Say what it is," we exhorted, saying with-
out saying it wasn't as bleak as it appeared. "Say it,"

we exhorted, "say what it is." Gray pervaded it so

                                            we

hated speech, all of it hate speech. How to say it with-
  out saying was our quandary, no matter we exhorted,
  "Say it," our call to her response, teeth twisting loose

                                      from

  our jaws… We said, "Say it," wanting Zvia not to,
  Nub's degree zero hate-say, split itness's I-and-I the
  it of it, we of that infection ourselves. We walked as

                                      if

the ground were unsteady, which it was, our way of
  not being on it never was but as our legs dictated, the
love book we wrote written by our feet. Dust caught in

                                    the

  hair on our legs and it coated our ankles, love's mind-
  edness ominous, dust-revelator light. Were we a band
or a gang we were set wondering, what drove us nos-
  talgia for past unrest or insecurity, precarity put away

                                    we

  drew back to, drawn-on lack of ground, guarantee…
  Who did it fall to to say we were set wondering, the
  it of it not the as-is of it, the as-if not yet tendered as

                                    such.

Zvia's discourse caught us headed uphill, out of breath,
  parched foothills off to both sides of us, thought no
sooner given than agreed with, yes, it was a GRADE OF

                                    DE-

SPOND we were on, the farther along we went the more
palpably uppercase, the farther along we went the worse
  we felt. A GRADE OF GOING OFF it might also have been,

                                    as

  if we did so asked what clime it was we'd come to, not to
let it smack of allegory but be as it was, only as it was, what it
  was, combustible brush on both sides of us, only as it was,

                                    the

  walk we were on only we
were on

•

Gray gave way to brown, Lone Coast foothills light
brown come summer, memory took us back to Lone
Coast. Memory a sort of possession it seemed, the
                                                    hav-
    ing of having had. Salt somehow had to do with
it, inland on the peninsula though we were, burnt-
    brown grasses underfoot as we walked, a telescope
                                                    dish
up the hill we were on... Zvia played muse for the
    occasion, calling it no special occasion. She wore sti-
letto heels on the inopportune terrain, not to be taken
                                                    al-
    legorically she said. She wore black silk, a kimono-
    like smock, temperature in the nineties no matter,
black silk absorbing the sun. It was only as it was we
    heard her say and we repeated after her. It was only as
                                                    it
    was we said... How she walked without her heels
going into the ground was a mystery at first, how she
    walked without stumbling or getting stuck. She walked,
we thought, only on the balls of her feet but that wasn't
                                                    so,
    the tips of her heels hit the ground we could see. An in-
    congruous music moved her up the hill we surmised,
the ubiquitous box lending her an escorting arm it lent us
                                                    as
well. We walked in the sideways Egyptian way. It might
    have been a pyramid whose wall we walked... It was
    a tune whose name lay on the tips of our tongues, beyond
                                                    re-
trieval, an iterative, permutating lick had hold of it. Only as
    it was of it as well she was now saying, all of it only as it
was and what it was. Only-as-it-was was the odd thing about
                                                    it.
    It was only as it was, what it was, we also said. An old
oak to our right seemed on the verge of speaking, so square-
    ly possessing the spot where it stood words might sure-
ly accrue to it we thought, we of the asymptotic tongue... So
                                                    we
    stopped and stood, out of breath, listening, the oak's axi-
    omatic speech the ubiquitous box's anonymous tune, what

respite there was an arid wind ruffling waist-high scrub. The

                                                            tel-
escope dish appeared also endowed with speech but not on the
  verge of it, withholding it Zvia went so far as to say, non-
allegorical she insisted, calling it the Star Cup even so. What
                                                           the
   dead rain portended an eventual spark bore skyward we
saw, the dish's non-allegorical say as tutorial as any. Only as
  it was no matter it was, we were on our way up on our way
                                                           out
we saw… We stood sipping from the Star Cup getting our
  breath back. Non-allegorical notwithstanding, we stood lift-
ing love's chalice we thought, a cast of mind we were no
                                                      time
   soon to cast off, each thing, it seemed, a satellite to itself.
We stood, during the lapse, not exactly knowing where we
  were and exactly not knowing where we were, a cast of mind
                                                   we
were no time soon to be done with, each thing, it seemed, the as
  of as it was. A certain logic, we were saying, would abide noth-
ing less, the as-it-was of it now a thing to be dealt with, this our
                                                  new
   say an incumbent say Zvia seconded, all call and response,
all antiphonal stitch… All this as much to wish on a straw as the
  it of as-it-was, sweat long since begun to roll down one's face
as the as of it, sweat spots dotting Zvia's black silk, black silk
                                                stick-
ing tighter to her shoulders, her breasts, her hips. London since
  left behind for Lone Coast, its hay-colored hills, hay-colored ra-
vines, hay-colored flats, I was thinking about my Dogon funeral.
                                                    This
  exact patch of earth I'll be said to've walked when I'm dead
I was thinking. *Zvia's glistening skin under black silk* I was think-
ing. *Her wet but astral body an imaginal stairway, a doorway*
                                                  of
sorts I was thinking. No special occasion though it was, we stood
transfixed for all time, unlikely launch on an otherwise humdrum
                                                sum-
  mer
day

Paint it flat was what we were to've done or painted
   flat was what we were to've been, acolytes of her
the very balls of whose feet were flat, no curvature, no
                                                    ac-
      cent to be had. A lesson in flatness it was or was to
   be but wasn't, not the relief stars gave it but a fixity
      of stars her blunt bodily address recruited. A counter-
point of sorts we sought instead… We were in the house
                                                    of
      the long tone without knowing it at first, what appeared
      to be flat part of a curved asymptotic run, ever so close
   it only feigned a flat course, a run we'd have called "So
                                                    Near,

   So Far" were the name not tak-
en

Flatness played a joke it seemed, Nub's new face-
lift so gone we called it Sag, the race vote of 2016
under its belt. It sent me seeking refuge in memory,

                                                    a
    certain summer, a certain line of scat, an elided col-
        lision... A certain black habit, habitual silk... It sent me
seeking my body's blunt distillery, Namoratunga's prom-
    enading stars... I lay prey to any curved recruitment, ever

                                                            so
    subtle notwithstanding, ever so tenuous, the ever ex-
tolled as-it-was and what-it-was of it, never to be known
    being taken hold of, contingency contingency's grasp,

                                                        grope,
    ghost

ITAMAR'S WHATSAID SAY BECOMING DEVOTIONAL

—"mu" two hundred fourth part—

We stood savoring Lone Coast salt, an incite-
ment, the schooled horns crooning offshore. Adobe
huts dotted our memory, Dogon granaries with
hats

on top. What had any of it to do with where we
stood we stood asking, salt's point or ping an in-
stigation again, salt's Atlantic portfolio tacking
west...

Itamar was telling me he found he took Zvia to
heart, a mere mask Sophia wore that she was no mat-
ter, consonant, he said, with lithe Eleanoir as well, her
chest

bone-close but its modest protrusions a thrill to one's
touch. "Ythmic admission honey's ooze at least," he
had said, "to lie, wounded leg to wounded hip," gray
day,

gray dateless adjournment. "It wasn't sight so much as
'scintillogy,'" he went on, "seen as if seen thru gas. 'Blur,
be what I am,' it clanged." There we stood, a two-headed
side-

show I thought. A periplum of sound we knew place by
nudged us leeward, to get to where the music was we
sought... The conditions for song did not exist but we
did

we assured ourselves, the offshore horns an illusion at
best, the conditions were not there but we were. We
had woken up flat but we were enjoying our time above
the

ground, finite though we knew it to be or so knew it
to be, to be alive was to be warned we already knew. We
had seen silhouettes under khaki, so resplendent soul
was,

only a glancing blow what it was. We had heard of
the wonders of wondrous midriff, seen and touched it our-
selves, all such amenity and more... Itamar's mistrust
of bodily life receded as he spoke of Zvia, to be in whose
pres-

ence was to be beset by spirit he said. Her luxurance of

hips. Her cropped hair. Her bare feet with painted toe-
nails an etymological glamor, girt knowledge, he said, gno-
sis, dark though in the open, dark wood metallic, dark

met-
al, Zvia the Magnetic One had come. Not long for bod-
ily favor he was afraid but, laws of touch abiding, pressed on…
The workings of waft he'd heard about as well and chose to

par-
take, the exact compact it and its other animated, the it of

it

it'd ever a-
gain

—————————————

A see-thru mystery he made of things I thought, that
  it was that was no mystery he sloughed it off say-
ing no sooner I mentioned it. We were up late reminisc-
ing the dead, deep in the cups music was and would
                                                al-
    ways be… Willie Hutch was on the box, the same
  song again and again, "Baby Come Home." He sat mourn-
  ing a lost love he never had. A night of male musing it
                                                was,
  come to include all etch, all abstract ambage, nought if
    not at Zvia's behest he made it seem, much more fraught
than felt I'd have said… My mother was a snake-fearing
                                                wom-
    an I said instead, my grandmother the same way with
      spiders. One foot in the grave he said it felt like and so
    on, one of the rickety elders now… So went our plutonic
                                                dia-
  logue, salvage we'd have
said

•

"Sad sacks," Itamar said catching our reflection in
   the sliding-door glass, Hutch on the box again,
Hutch what time it was all night. Music for reflection
                                                    it
   was as we sat drinking, thinking, so at risk was our
hold on any of it, ourselves not least of all. We sat mourn-
   ing a loss we didn't have he sang about so bittersweetly
                                                    we
      wished it our own, an intuitive book we beat bent on
   preaching. We were alright we kept saying, man talk.
      He'd be okay Itamar said, ignoring the pain in his leg…
We sat blinded by something it seemed, the daylit ghost
                                                    we'd
      seen perhaps, ripped inside out we'd have said were
      there a difference, as light as life itself it seemed. Was
   it a male horizon we were hemmed in by we sat won-
      dering as if we gnawed on burnt bacon, burnt toast, our
                                                    sto-
      machs long since anyone's but ours. We were alright
   we kept saying even so, man code, such alrightness as the
      saying belied, so unprompted it was, we were alright or
                                                    we'd
   be alright we said again and again… We chewed our burnt
      bacon and toast, shot the breeze all the while expecting
      we'd make a move. "Biding our time" was the way we put
                                                    it,
      no matter what was at issue remained unknown. To be
   was to be summoned we knew but to what we were loath to
      say. The piano's drop sound at the start was at us again,
                                                    how
      they did it, how it could ever be done, we marveled at
   yet again, the clink of it like ice cubes hitting glass… Next
      I knew he was back talking about Zvia, the raw devotion
   pear-bottom hips and her midriff elicited made rare, apprised
                                                    of
      some further front one tended toward. Bodily sag's intimat-
   ed way, wrack chapel. Churchical he called it, girth ab-
   sconditus, would-be grasp. It was Zvia who had left he all
                                                    but
      moaned, lamented, Zvia Hutch, he said, sang about. "All
   my life," he said, weary, then he said, "All night long," an an-

them or an oath it seemed, an oath or an anthem of sorts, of

                                                             sorts

and as well a sort of
sigh

Mr. P, Sneaky Pete of late, leaned in, there but
   not there. I felt our hands were tied behind our
 backs, grasp absconditus etched in the very air,
                                              bod-
   ily embrace athwart bodiless exit, our days not
 unnumbered we knew. Churchical girth sprang
   philosophic oath, sigh, anthem, a mystico-romantic
 sough wherewith Itamar's lament grew devotional...
                                              Willie

   sang for us all he said, himself, unbeknown to him-
   self, singing, the say of it the singing Willie sang, he
 said, for us... Zvia was the one who had gone, the
                                              la-
   mented one, he sang, Mr. P's puppet I thought,
   Mr. P leaning in like never before. An inside lining
   ran the length of Lone Coast, a fold or a pocket
                                           Mr. P
   lay stowed away in, salted, I said, away in, the Lone
                                           Coast

   salt we savored
 his

•

(chant)

Thinking beyond were there beyond to think, we
   discovered thinking made it so, thought maybe
   thinking wasn't all that made it so, love's close
                                       aro-
   mas, we knew, odorous but for love. Zvia with-
drew her arms from around what would one day
   not be there we also knew, love's anointed waist
                                    pulled
   away from, no one's if not his own Itamar let
out, an oath, a sigh, an anthem of sorts... Her very
   sweat a fine perfume he attested, Hutch's piano
intro egged him on. A new tenderness it made for
                                 hoar-
   sened his voice it seemed or he made it seem, the
   offshore horns onshore he made it seem, sprinkled
on by meddlesome salt. None other than Mr. P's
                                rid-
   dlesome salt I whatsaid, put in what otherwise
went unsaid. "Please, please, Mr. P," I wanted to say
   but I bit my tongue. Mr. Preemption he might've
                              been,
   the what-sayer's what-sayer, everything subject
to intervention, nothing self-sufficing anymore...
   Itamar was Baul by now, Bengali, his oath or his an-
them an arrow stuck in a cloud. Rain came down I'd
                              have
   said but Mr. P blocked it, the P of impediment now.
   Itamar let out how he hurt from his hip to his ankle,
the it-of-its deep assembly whose ache he'd redeem
                             some-
   way, man talk's ythmic pretense. The offshore horns
were now onshore Mr. P had me say, their onshore sound
   an old, gravid sound, shaken ground we'd have walked
                              had
   we up and gone, legs and feet in deep league with
Zvia's gray paint, some elsewhere we averred we'd be.
   Otherwise we breathed in, breathed out, the offshore
                             horns
   ushered us on... We sat drinking and thinking amid

the sea lions' cries off Lone Coast, the offshore horns
a palliative of sorts. By now his whole body hurt he
                                                    said,
    hurt's distillation an oath or an anthem, all the harm
done done so innocently he thought, better there were
    evil he thought. He and Zvia had opened an orphanage
                                                        he
    said, the children's high cries an aria of sorts, an oath
he heard sworn by the salt in the wind he said, salt's
grain never to be dispensed with, the grain, he said, he
took it all with, man talk again… Mr. P told me tell him
                                                        salt
    would out, the cry of the abandoned boys and girls wo-
    ven with it, say thread was a wind of sorts. Denizen
of none but windy places, purveyor of quandary and qualm,
    Itamar himself might have been Mr. P. The way her body
                                                        grew
broad with the years murdered him he said. "Please, please,
    Mr. P," I went to say but it came out edited. "A dove with no
    branch in its beak flew by," I said instead, "branch" code for
                                                        cau-
    tion, "dove" code for puppet, "flew" code for something
    whose meaning I missed… Heterotopic I wanted to call it, the
    it-outside-itself I knew to be true, Zvia some Everywoman
                                                        it
seemed… Itamar shook off my suggestion before I made it,
    read my mind it seemed, his voice going hoarse with the ar-
    dor she called up, sense compacted of mist and uncertainty,
                                                        car-
oling's clime soon
come

It was what some would have called Long Night
Lounge, Willie Hutch unremitting on the box. I
was what some would have known as the what-
sayer... Was it Sophia doffing her Zvia mask he

                                         meant
and lamented I'd've asked had Mr. P not hijacked
  my tongue. What was devotion devoted to I asked
instead, Mr. P's mouthpiece... "The pear-bottom

                                   reviv-
  al tent," Itamar said, "the ocean in it," after which
all there was were seagulls blown around by the wind
  as waves broke on the shore, salt savor never to be

                                   gotten

off our lips, our nostrils, our
tongues

SONG OF THE ANDOUMBOULOU: 225½

—dionysius live at the apollo—

We were most a nation with James Brown
  on one knee at the Apollo, the closest
we got him saying, "I'm so weak." All our
                  ways
  and means a lost someone, all our wishing
one, the closest we came was when he screamed
  and we screamed, we of the public swoon...
                      It was
James Brown on the box when it wasn't Hutch,
a pimped or impeded walk from one gray state
  to another, the weak-kneed aggregate we formed
or fell in with or the palatial pea coat Andreannette
                        wore,
  Zvia's gloss on whom we gave hardly a thought...
Nation time time athwart time, having had a black
  president not even close, Dionysius gone Apollonian
                    the
  closest we got. All the grieving distance held at arm's
  length gone over again, having had a black presi-
dent not it at all but Crater made us pay. We stood or
                  we
  sat buffeted from gray to gray, never a nation more
than when we yelled, "Sing your song," or yelled, "Go
  on, scream," never more than as it got cold outside,
                na-
  tion time time athwart time... The one word kept
echoing, "someone," nation having nothing to do with
  it but common, close but not really, meta maybe it
                  was.
  The way the bottom dropped out of it so spoke to
us we winced, never a nation more than unsupported,
  never a nation more than gasping, "Help me somebody,"
more nation the more needy we were. More nation the
                  more
  Dionysian we were, the more Dionysian the more the
  Apollo was our White House, the Flames our Con-
gress, never more nation than when the nation let us go...
                  We

were never more Dionysian than at the Apollo, each of
us Dionysius live at the Apollo, our nation not anoth-
er nation but another kind of nation. We were most a nation
when the trumpet cut like a blade and we screamed our

                                                    throats

raw, never more a nation than when we accepted the
reed's insinuation. Our nation not another nation but anoth-
er kind of nation, we were free to submit and submitting

                                                    un-

bound, true of no nation we
knew

The box being what it was, I might've been any-
where, place was of little consequence to me. The
box being what it was, I was in love of late but

                                        what
    to stand on unsure. Crater was all the rage, eve-
ryone hurt but taking it in, like something we
    ate ripped at our stomachs but we were hungry,

                                    no
way could we stop, the box being what it was be-
    side the point... The box being what it was, we
blew loose. Light would abide and time would tell we

                                        knew,
    made out like we knew, so making out, we found,
made it so, another index amending *The Book of So.*
Might love be polis's bond, even lust, better that than
commerce the moving hand wrote... We were the High

                                        Boys,
Itamar and I, I Insofar-I, fraught string filled our heads.
    We were national, never more so than when we blew,
    oboes we'd have been had we been axes, high would

                                        what
    we came
to

SONG OF THE ANDOUMBOULOU: 226

—scratch point meditation—

I lay pondering the trace I'd leave, the whence
and the wherefore yet to be made out, musing's
  radix a toss of water I thrashed in, many a move
                           the
   wrong move I thought. Mystery might mean
doom I was thinking, requiem ever the note one's
  tongue went toward, tears on our cheeks hot,
                         can-
dle wax. I wanted to say something that would
  sum Nub up, legs out from under me as the tide
slid in, the abandoned boy and girl come to what…
                       They'd
  be treating themselves to self-medicine I thought,
a thought that woke me up. The tide was my falling
  asleep I found out, snapped out of it by the thought,
                      one's
   inner body up to no good I thought. Thought crept
along, thought kept me up, not knowing, late whistles
  gone off, nonstop. The din it made made me think,
thought's benefit in doubt notwithstanding. I began to
                     be
  thought's remand… All the same, I dreamt I sat on the
  dock of a lake with Andreannette, pant legs rolled
up, bare feet in the water. We talked all day, talked into
                     the
  night, husk in our voices come from under. Or was
it Netsanet I sat with and talked with I wondered, no
  longer sure, thought's prize and thought's precipice her
                       do-
main. I lay recalling her contour's meditative remit, the be-
  ginnings of the remnants of what light rebutted cover,
part muse, part grade school teacher. Dogs outside were
                     bark-
  ing, ducks quacking, the menagerie whichever she was
had inducted us into waking up, dailiness's new day begun…
  So a waking song I saw and said it would be, whatsay
                     nev-
  er not a part or apart from it. Let net be the name that

might be either I decided, net be the name that might
be both. It was all one to me which was which or who

                    was

who I decided. I wanted now to say nothing that would
sum it all up, net less thread than opening, net more not

                   than

was it was
clear

       •

Having come back to Scratch Point I was talking
more to myself it seemed, an Insofarian side-
step, away what advance there was, my say-hey

            jubi-

lance gone away. I was pondering the time
bombs our bodies had become, we who'd once
been young, tired of the tease it all had been.

            I was

noticing how out of our way we went, the way
words were a detour we took, music even more.
I was noticing it all the more, noticing my next de-
tour... I was noticing how detour might have agreed

            with

contour, Scratch Point dispensary the gist of their
concordance, everything itself yet something else.
So it was I stood pat as pat parted ways with itself,

            such

the way of things at Scratch Point. I stood inured
to the wind blowing out, the seagull droppings on
the rock I stood on, the chill spray all that way north

            up

Lone Coast, nothing not what I was told it would be...
What I was noticing was contour-as-pocket, not so
much noticing as considering it, pocket's claim on

            con-

tour one's wanting it to keep, keep's parted way con-
tour's collapse. I stood pat, going nowhere, Scratch
Point's Immanuel Kant, my critique of pure anything all

            it

was, all of it losing time I was noticing, all of it lost
to time. Time-as-would-be-pocket-would-be-purse I was
noticing, keep's promise coin I considered, would-be

            keep.

Time's would-be pocket I was noticing reconsidered,
   time's pocket's would-be purse… I was Scratch Point's
Parmenides it seemed. It was all one to me what any of
                                                              it
   was. I stood bestride myself standing pat, horse and rid-
   er. Bestride was to all but be beside myself I noticed,
                                                    net's

   Insofarian
catch

Switched off another unbearable newscast.
  It was all one, compliance or complaint, Nub's
deep state deep numbness, I at I's' expense…
                                        Non-
    Insofarian I's realm it was, the monad's last
  call or stand or both, a dead ear to the beckoning
    living, a deaf ear to the beckoning dead… The
                                        husk
      in our voices would abide I told myself, rasp's
    raw truth a prolegomena, thesis teased out from
      all our mishandling, a crude insistent something no
                                        way
      with which to be done… Scratch Point ran from our
        feet unimpeded, point-to-plane's everyday miracle, a
                                        drive
        to the water's edge
        and back

I stood pondering the recondite calm raging
   around me, the proverbial point it started
from. Scratch Point's namesake abrasion, Scratch
  Point's namesake spear, sand and sun ray were
                                 all
   there ever was, whence's wherefore but for
  what I could make of it, making it more ythmic
  still... I stood on tenuous cartilage, tenuous
                             bone.
My face was made of rubber, I was Miss Betty's
  boy, my mouth so elastic sound sought refuge, a
                           philos-
  ophic damping's de-
  mur

WE THE MIGRATING THEY AGAIN

—"mu" two hundred sixth part—

Not a reading people just a right one, right
  with God, they said of themselves, not to be
of the book but be the book. We were on the
                             far
  side of Ool-Ya-Koo, the lately opaque den-
    izens of which they were. They were a
book the book was being thrown at. Fanning
                           blow-
  back against the rookie head of state they were
accused of. We ran into them on the run. They
  were their own ythm, not someone's myth, they
                            said,
  Nub's new scaremonger mask no matter. Were
they we the migrating they again we queried,
  ours no more than Nub's they answered, no…
                          The
  outskirts of Ool-Ya-Koo fell away to the west,
    badlands dotted with low-lying scrub, tenuous pro-
scenium, dry run. We were west of the Euphrates,
                       west
  of the Mississippi, west of every river in the
world. Were they we the migrating they we asked
  again, no such book as a book of so for them it
                    ap-
peared, except it be such as they were. Nub's col-
  lapse into Crater lay on all our lips, theirs the migrat-
  ing buzz ours as well. Were they we the migrating
                     they
we asked again… A piano broke down at the back of
  our thoughts, a tune the dent in whose head proved
  essential, the way we the migrating they stood still.
                    The
  ground itself in flight, they were the oldtime people
camouflaged amid the elements. It was a wonder we
  could make them out, expiration a membrane away at
                   all
  points, the omen borne moment to moment, the o-
men momentariness was. They spoke without cease of

an inside singer, God's counterpart in the tone world

                                       we

took it, the book there'd've been had there been one,
  they themselves the book there was... Bodily abidance
not be all there was we begged, bodily breakdown sprung.
                                        Bod-

  ily breakdown Pentecost of a kind, we went on, every
such petition the we the migrating they they were, they the
                                        mi-

  grating
we

Could what the inside singer sang have been
    called a far cry we'd have called it that, an ec-
topic TV what window there was. We were

                                        try-
    ing not to see it somehow, not sure what
        we heard was there, asking what they could
    tell us about the inside singer's timbre, asking

                                        what
        it would take to get us there... The faint piano
    we'd heard before drifted in again, neither hav-
        ing ended nor begun but always there we intuited,

                                        an
    awayness vaguely bruited about. What to say, what
        to say, we pounded the heels of our hands to-
gether asking, kids clamoring for candy we might've
been... What to say was awayness itself... What

                                        to
    say was exactly their theyness, we the migrating
    they they no longer were, a gradual release it turned

                                        out
to be

•

Ool-Ya-Koo stretched away forever, a gift or
   a giving way of ground at our feet, an avidity of
  place we had or would have none of, "Cover,"
                                we
   brayed, "be done." We were nothing if not we
the migrating they, cloud country truly our country,
  rasp our country, "Cover, be done," though we
                             pled…
   The ground fell away, forgetful, indifferent,
  theirs, had they thought it so, no more. Let all be
   brought to light they demanded. We could reckon
ourselves exported into them we imagined, reckon
                            them
   imported into us, a suspect symmetry no sooner
    thought than rejected, what lay beyond reckoning
drew us on. All the bluffs and plateaus grew pensive, a
  tangle of prospecti lived and unlived, the they that
                           were
crowding our memory the right, not-reading ones, a-
   live by their lights, benighted by ours. The buttes
  and the mesas fell away, lost in thought, Ool-Ya-Koo
                         se-
   ceding from Nub if it could, we the mutating dead…
Or was it the land of Oo-Bla-Dee we were in we kept
   wondering, a scratch or a skip, a nicked-up record put
                            us
   there, a staticky flat we trekked across. We asked as
    much, "Oo-ba-dilia-la-bin-doo. Is this the land of Oo-
Bla-Dee?" All the migrating they we asked answered
                         yes
   except one, who of the others, meaning too ready
to concede, said, "They too light," meaning less inside
   than out, his the heavy take he said, the inside sing-
  er's take, he said we were nowhere if not Ool-Ya-Koo,
                         Oo-
   Bla-Dee an entirely other place… He sang a song, an
   inside song he told us, that they acquired by way of
  tenuous bodies a taste for tenuousness, a theme the inside
                             sing-
   er was known to
expound

●

Low Forest lushness a memory, kudzu-covered
   woods a green cathedral we reminisced, pianism
  spoke low but more beseechingly, that there be

                                     speech
   seeping up from underground. What it spoke
 disavowed itself, let itself be spoken, the awayness
  it also was and wanted to get to thus gotten, an

                                a-
 mendment otherwise underfoot… We were begin-
  ning to be aware of this. We were beginning to
know the bodily envelope for what it was, ourselves

                                not
   there but there, the same for them, we the migrat-
ing they both ways. We were beginning to see Ool-Ya-
Koo's evaporative élan, see and also be it, beginning

                                  to
   bid all amplitude goodbye… Was it a spook sona-
ta we wondered, a too-soon ensemble, the whatsaid
  arrivancy we saw. We were losing what we had but

                                 in
 a cumulative way, we dreamt, kept it, a commemora-
  tive ruse by way of which we trudged on. I was of like
persuasion, one of the we. I was wounded and I wanted

                              wis-
   dom to accrue, the gash in my leg a beneficence the
 way it was in the lore I leaned on… Had we had them
 we'd have blown trumpets, spoken thru mutes, low-spo-
ken say an assemblage of deferrals and feints, a sense of

                              lived
 life underneath it, a temptation to allegorize turned away…
  One wanted to cross one's heart and swear something…
One wanted to believe, one wanted to be a believer… The

                              old-
  time people looked
on

(22.v.17: angle)

    Came of late to imagine Eleanoir my Layla.
Were we east or west I wondered, the comb-
  over sprouting corn in the land of beheadings,
decapitism's namesake fruit. Were we in the
                                     Ba-
hamas I wondered, B'Head's kingdom. My
  head rolled and came to rest at Eleanoir's feet,
between her feet, bodiless but with eyes for bod-
  ily largesse. It lay dreaming Eleanoir commando
                                  under
  a sundress, dreaming it looked up her dress… This
that there be a plot one could work in, work and re-
  work… That there be heat seeping up from under, all
                                     else

afoot

Groove Holmes's "Misty" was on the box,
jump summons, a blow to my rolling head.
  I made the leap Eleanoir being Layla would
                                    be,
    the one balm the migrating they cast back...
  I hid my head under her dress, the world was
    falling apart. I seceded, now of unlike persua-
sion, no longer one of the we... I was there but
                                    not
    there. According to some, I sang my head off.
                                    To be
    yet of the book but
  not

The receding we grew one with the ground
   as it flew, we the rotating day's dark facet,
athwart what stuck reprise we went caught
                                   in,

   Ool-Ya-Koo's vocables remiss. It was all
only refuge we sought, they sought, all open-
   ing out toward the tone world, the world whose
immigrants we'd be. All of it going away as we
                                    lost

   what grip we had, gotten could a scream have
   gotten it we reckoned, flown beyond reckoning
                                we

knew

I awoke as before asking what would the
   day bring. "Night sat me down" was what
my hit head chimed, reeling's way yet to be
                              done.
   Bell rung, I let the bid of sleep linger. My
     passage back I let myself take slowly, a
   human-headed hawk on my neck… Would I
                          were
in Egypt I sighed, would I drove an ox cart past
   a water wheel again, would it were back be-
fore Nub conjured Crater. But what did I know I
                        won-
   dered, what light not commemorative light, can-
dle-bearing boats we pushed into a river, minia-
   ture boats we let go out to the sea… I put Groove
                        on
   the box, the House of the Hammond B-3 my
only hope. I stood repelling the new drift of things,
   attempting to. Leg let me down, Ba stood me up,
no one wanting to hear about soul anymore, no one if
                        not
   me I thought. Earland was up next, a psalm against
   time, "More Today Than Yesterday" nothing if
not mine, nothing if not a millionth repeat… We'd
                    be
raising our hands to our mouths in shock I'd wok-
   en up thinking. Met by more talk of the moment,
   no talk more extravagant, somewhere a genuine
                     mo-
   ment lived I thought. Moment might be all we
had I thought, moment more than only its own for-
   feiture. I was thinking what to make of the day
in such manner, erstwhile amends or merely erstwhile
                    eva-
   sion… Les McCann was next up, the House of the
   Happy Right Hand. Moment might be more than it-
self I thought, no moment not stolen the sense of it I
   got, thought so inured of itself it braved emptiness, an
                    in-
   stigant so blithe a way it went. I was awake not yet

knowing what day it was or what it would bring, what to
do with it, was it mine to do anything with, the onflow
                                                    of
    it not suggesting that, not suggesting not. The is-ness
of it, such as it presumably was, went without saying,
    what exactly I went on doing were thought-say a kind
                                                    of
doing, itself nonsay of a
sort

                        •

    Hard getting out of bed but for the project of be-
ing present, the now there kept being buzz about,
    the moment we were exhorted to be in. Could one
                                                ever
    be out I woke up wondering, the now having been
what it was I was in even as I slept, a pod of con-
    currence I thought. I stared out at what looked like
                                                a
picture in a book but, no book but were it a book of
    the book's preclusion, there was no book… I thought
back on the migrating they, the right but not reading
                                                ones,
    their book, might it be said to be one, their being
the book, so one with the moment their thought. Thus
    to so fully be was what they meant by being right
                                                with
God I thought, more thought than they'd have given
    it, so coincident with it they were. I was asking what
to make of reflection, looking out without reflection
                                                be-
    fore a window I looked right thru, one with what I
saw it seemed, asking without reflection my answer
    to reflection, awake to the day being made… I stood
                                                re-
    flectionless, the text or the testimony simply stand-
ing was, one of the migrating they the we I was one
    of were, we the migrating they crux and candle, boats
borne out to sea. What to make of the day receded, fell
                                                a-
    way, jammed-up question the day itself answered, a

world out the kitchen window I was in… So easily an-
swered it seemed I saw there was no question, what to

                                          make
of the day the day's making so meek an equation it fell

                                               a-

way as
well

The blue sky lay like bloom over Low Forest, mo-
mentariness like a pall. The much talked about
moment loomed impalpable, evaporative as it went
                                                    by.
   I was wondering did all moments live on some-
where, there to be gotten hold of some way. I was
   wondering were they forever undone, looking out the
window as a fox darted into the woods... I was awake
                                                    stand-
   ing over the kitchen sink now, nowhere if not thought's
   own city, Les's happy hand in my ear. I was in the
moment trying to be in the moment, in the moment if I
                                                    tried
   or not... No moment not taken away I stood thinking,
wondering what salvage there was, thinking what con-
   torted way one thought to connive it, time against time's
                                                    re-
call

ANUNCIO'S THIRTEENTH LAST LOVE SONG

—"mu" two hundred eighth part—

Toward the end we lived a bodiless life.
  Anuncia kept sorrow at bay as I lay
busted up. I was feeling more alive than
                         ever
  even so, more alive albeit or because
life had grown strange, what was left of
  bodily life gone waftless, no musk floated
our way… I lay observing a lilac's routine
                      mira-
  cle, opening as it did, seeming to say, of
    all things, it would never die. Anuncia
turned and walked away. I noticed the lengthen-
ing sag of her buttocks, bodiless though we
                   both
  were, the far side of bodily draw. A certain
something I saw words would not accrue to
  I also noticed, something I took to be seeming
                    it-
  self, a certain something seeming nothing or
nothing in particular, the potential to seem, noth-
  ing more… New terror attacks were on the TV
                at
  the foot of the bed, the world busted up like me.
  Seeming's attack on seeming I said let's call it,
more to myself than to Anuncia though she heard it,
                  bod-
  iless though we continued to be. What manner of
realm were we in we couldn't help wondering, love's
  evident flight merely one of its provocations, what
                man-
  ner and what put us there… An intergalactic dust
intervened I thought, no sooner thought than saw
  it so clearly I rubbed my eyes and looked again,
               eve-
  ry kiss of late a kiss good-
bye

·

I was hearing the flow of music thru time, the
same headache over the ages. I heard a circle of
  beakless cardinals caroling light beyond audition,
                                                    ma-
    larial hush calling it all a contrivance, nothing
  offered up otherwise. I was caught by surprise
    by it ending, then caught by surprise again, Anun-
cia standing again at the bed's edge... I lay imagining
                                                    what
      leaving my body would be like, bodiless though we
      already were, our being so a test or a foretaste I won-
  dered, taking between my thumb and my index finger
    the hem of her dress. Moot proof it amounted to were
                                                    it
proof at all, everything known to be a construct, noth-
    ing itself anymore... I was remembering Anuncia's
    perfumed cleavage, remembering not reminiscing,
                                                    not
    forgetting we were bodiless, the boon it was. I was
remembering the night she first bestowed her favors,
    not reminiscing but remembering the it of it, bearing
                                                    down
      knowing now there was an it of it, bodiliness's ruin
    our redoubt. My sinuses were filled with glue, food
    sat bubbling on my stomach, all of it abstract, a meta-
physical complaint, qualms afflicted drums, as were
                                                    we...
    Qualm thought's thought of itself I said let's call it,
thought's metaphysical conceit. I was feeling the way
    the light moved inside the hem of Anuncia's dress, my
                                                    in-
    dex finger and thumb hold-
ing on

My worsening hip no longer in the way, I walked
　　unencumbered could it be called walking what
I did, all the jitteriness of gusting air, winded remit.
　　　　　　　　　　　　　　　　　　　　　The

　　boon being bodiless was I was newly learning...
　　　I was in school, even back in school, *memory vs.*
reminiscence an inequation written on the board,
　　Anuncia my school-teacher muse. We were sheer
　　　　　　　　　　　　　　　　　　　　mind

　　again, freed of our sagging skin. Thinking's own
　　habitude, we loved each other's thoughts, each the
　　　　　　　　　　　　　　　　　　　　　oth-

　　er's prodigy, precocious cohort,
kin

•

(chant)

Citizen vs. denizen an inequation we came to
as well, the TV on lest we miss the latest out-
rage. Anuncia took me in under the smock she
                                                    no
    longer wore, bodily need for cover long since
gone. She escorted me into rarified air, mere
air, air what before had been tissue and bone,
                                        love's
    exact quiddity, suchness I said let's call it, such-
ness Anuncia concurred. We had been a vio-
lin played like a sarangi, fibrousness and rasp all
                                                    there
    was, all body was. We were nothing but pertur-
bation the air underwent... My fingers and my
    palms cupped Anuncia's cheeks but for bodiless-
ness, not-having's way of having mine to learn.
                                            Bod-
    ily retreat gotten to, time taken, we were living
a timeless life, the bond it wouldn't always be.
Slack demeanor we at one time wore fell away,
                                            the
    mystic assembly breath and bone were revealed
to be. Not a divine but a demiurgic tryst Anuncia
    said let's call it, warbling I'd have sworn I heard,
                                                    bird
lore gotten of late... All it was was we were in Aire-
    gin it occurred to me, music's two-way topos,
anagrammatic stoop, elongated stop. We were in
                                            and
    of the book, the book itself, lexicality's permuta-
ble drift, the migrating they we also were. By the
time it was gotten down it was gone, the book what
                                                    no
    longer was. Between book's end and bed's edge
we tarried, late light exquisitely strung it so upheld us,
    beginning to bid our bodies goodbye, bone good-
bye, aggravated body and bone. It was all moving on,
                                                    we
    with it, Anuncia's teacherly girth mere memory, air

our valedictory embrace… Had we bodies we'd have
sidled up to one another, stood closer were we stand-
ing, sat closer were we sitting, crossed legs were we

                                                                     lying

down. What we'd have done had we bodies we'd al-
ready done. Air had become all thrum, body had be-
come all edge, what cut. Smoke hung over Crater. It

                                                             was

all toward the end, to what end we were unclear. Horse-
hair. Sirening string… Was it air was only its image
we wondered, mind alone, floating free, image a mirage I

                                                            won-

dered, had we bodies, bodies of air all we were. Toward
the end we were only so much breath, were we that. "Call
it virtuality's precinct," Anuncia whispered, hoping to take

                                                            the

edge off the worked-up air we flew. "Thought's own prin-
cipality," she added, the thought of which put us over, the
we she insisted we'd be, albeit bodiless, the way not-having

                                                            had

with us, possessed… The true heroes of air it would be
we wanted to be, aerial spirit. Pure impending was all it was
we strove to be, what what had been bodies wanted to be,

                                                            the

falling away finding our
way

_____

At song's end we went on singing, a fugue slip into
    hymnal out of bed's edge, not so much a last as
a lasting song. We were wanting to be remembered,
                                                    air
    no matter we were, not yet light we were. Scraps
      and a record of scuffle verified the law, that there
was an ocean one was only a drop in, onliness's
                                              one-
    drop rule... We were wanting to be among the
remembered, no matter a weakening polis, words or
    shades of feeling no one knew. We were a part of
                                              the
world's adornment or would be, bodiless though we
    were, naked had we bodies, airs yet to have been, had
                                              we

been

Could we kiss without lips, embrace without bod-
    ies, negation's impossible proof. We pervaded the
realm we were in, the realm we were, the leafless
                                                    *Book
    of So*... Who touched us touched anything but, the
anywhere else we'd be. Thought's decree, thought's
    desiderata, platonic or plutonic we'd be... So near, so
                                                        far,
    no difference. Both it
    turned out we'd
be

THIRD ÉTUDE ENDING "SOON COME" REBEGUN

—"mu" two hundred ninth part—

We were a search party the next time out. We
   scouted retribution and remunerative states
we would all pass thru, try though we might to
                            rise
   above. Sprung similitude put us on parallel
tracks. Allegory might've been its name but
   it wasn't. To make it mean something was our
                            aim.
   To make it mean was to make it more real,
     more than real, real abound itself... We came
to a moonlit stretch, dry scrub underfoot, those
                         known
   as the flown ones down for the night. They lay
dreaming about the bodies of the proper ones, a new
   notion come into their heads, a new recognition
                         while
they slept, spawn of a tribe yet to come. We lay
   the same, we saw, parallel and spied upon, people
of the pulse, the broken song's high cry, seeds, it
                         ap-
   peared, eaten by sparrows... Blown away by
wind if not washed away by water, sprung recon-
naissance ran its course, new reconnoiter. We
were back to where we camped in no time, psychic
                         flight
   alone what carried us it occurred to us, a thought we
   took back, disproven by the bramble and the burrs
on our socks... Threads of light came down, gowns
                         of
   light. The moon drew beauty from reticence, blood
     from its pale presentation. Another sonic sphere
   cried out. The wonder of thread was we were naked
                         un-
   derneath, Hofriyati, wonder yet to be gotten over...
We feasted ahead of time on condolences, moot solace
                         to
   come, soon
come

•

Words came from forty-some years before, words
 not given then given now. We camped on a slope,
the slightest incline ever, womanly amplitude an
                                        image
 of the earth we fell asleep dreaming, a meadow
above a meadow above a lake. It lay inland from
Lone Coast we knew, north of Lone Coast, the
reach of the world as clean as ice or an edge of chill
                                        as
 cold as crystal, edge to be taken off, drape or em-
 brace… A gangly symmetry bound it together, the
it of it remanding the was of it, Lone Coast, Crater
                                        Lake,
 names not given now given. It all hung together
in an offhand way we were thinking, happy to've
 come to see it so, happy to see anything at all we
                                        lay
so blinded. It was a state we had no name for, felic-
 ity's romp and ranging forth an astute glue, backs
given the contours of the ground we lay against… We
                                        were
 the flown ones, we'd have been plucked featherless,
 drape against undress the galactic war the proper ones
fought, our dreams of their bodies the planets. Comets.
                                        Mag-

 netic
light

———————————

We had pitched our tents, not so much pitched as
popped. We thought ourselves blessed to be there
   feeling it, whatever the feeling might be, deliberate

                                              ex-

   penditures of breath, long breathers between…
We were in a mood for study. We lived inside skin
   looking out pores wide as windows. Not since

                                          Ita-

mar and Sophia studied each other had blood run
   so hot, not since we all first paired off, sat face to
face, legs open, erogenies abroad in the gap, yogic

                                          stet…

   The moon drew blood thru induction, pear-squat
inertia, whatever motor there was… We went farming

                                              our

      heads all
   night

•

Fabric vs. fold was the inequation we were now
being taught. The night sky had a matte, muted look.
Crater Lake lay so clear we saw to the bottom, no

                                                  water

was in it. We were learning how the past bled
into the present, the present bled into the past, team-
taught by stars, bramble, brush. Deep study some
said. I was one of them. Breathing in to breathe back

                                                 out,

landing elsewhere, the lip of a canyon water cut a-
cross the world. Ours or another, abided with or
abetted by, deep study breathing out to breathe back

                                                 in…

Reentry we were called, we kept landing elsewhere.
Nocturnal tillage, we the nightly farmers, heaven-
ly rubes. We were kissing the world goodbye, a throwa-
way clime, high-crime climate, we the galactic eldren.

                                                 We

slept deep enough needing to pee was no problem, wet-
ting ourselves as we slept. Wet fold, wet fabric, the
turning to what was at hand, what lay dependent, that

                                                 of

which much had been said, whiling away eternity,
fingertipped eternity's end… Night's late whatsay, vale-
dictory we could see, lamenting what would be done
to the world. We were stumbling but still above ground,

                                               the

Field of Reeds messed up. We were singing the death
of the earth, deep study, getting ready to be gone. We
were conflating the two, caroling dearth, some common

                                             con-

ceit we broke
down to

Our campfire blown on by wind bore witness, the
wood of the world red, yellow, orange, lit up.
An iron grate we fell thru burning bore in as well,
                                                    we
the white ash we studied, woebegone but to know
    what soul was... An Armenian wind blew thru my
femur, Eskenian on the box my head had become. I
                                                stared
    into the fire, my aunt looking down to see both her
legs gone. A lifted ember sparked, spoke, the wood
    of the world ascending, all the shrill wind's insistence,
                                                    mere

    sometimey
wind

Dream synonymy's drummed-up equation,
  Edge and Estelle who before had been
Ed and Stella. It was its way of saying what
                         was
  otherwise too crude, one and yet another
phantom cut, my aunt's lost legs... The meta-
  meadow we were trying to get to above the
                                 lake
  was as well. Clear Lake we now called it,
  redolent of youth. Down the hill we all went.
  We slid sitting on flat cardboard boxes, flatten-
ing the weeds and the grasses as we went. We
                             were
  dream-taught, taken to school, each of us un-
    der the mere wind's tutelage, each of us given
a blow-thru bone... Death itself lay close to our
                           lips
  as we blew, tremulous reed we could barely
hold on to, tremulous reed we each amounted to,
    shaken by the reed we shook. We slid inside a
                         field
so immense it all went foggy, a lighted fog streaked
  where the sun sat behind it, a fit of paint we sat
inside painted inside out... I stared into the fire, logs
                             go-
  ing gray and white, Edge and Estelle the way I dealt
without dealing, nominal stay, nominal study, dream
                           syn-
  onymy's late
  retort

I invoked Our Lady of Amputees, not knowing
was there one, reminiscing flat weeds and grass-
es, back when we were beautiful youth. I'd have
launched a worldstopping song were there one, an

over-
song, even a half oversong, close to the bone I
blew or blew into, song said to be of the An-
doumboulou, song, spoken or sung, long since, all

even-
tually ash I
knew

Brother B floated north of the lake, disparity's
  own host, awake as with one eye shut. "Tell
me true," he remembered Zvia requesting, a wish
                                                to

    make wish disperse. Tell, he despaired, was
  what the is of it would not do, lest is take itself
    to be telling, he thought, thinking it thru, tell-
ing to the side of all need to tell further, the is and
                                                the

    it of it one... The lake lay, clarity's riposte. The
    forest thinned out on its way to the lakeshore,
  verge's true liege, legendary love, Brother B reflect-
  ed, mold of what could not but have been to come.
                                            Light's

    bequest lay echoing, a baroque tonal reflux, tint
  and articulate tincture, Brother B's liquid remit. I
    regarded it the not yet beloved lake, my blue meta-
  physical sweet tooth's retreat, a naïve hold of water
                                                gla-

    cial happenstance explained... We heard water
  where we knew there was water announced without
    accent, the is I'd have wished it would be. Broth-
  er B, knowing that, grew worshipful. Noise had given
                                                way

    to an older amenity, wood no longer thorn if not pet-
    al, the flown ones' herbivorous roost where the lone
  ones gathered... A loose, low-to-the-ground muscling
                                                pre-
vailed

                        •

    It was the lore of lakes more than the lake that mat-
    tered or that mattered as much at least. All our
  lives we'd heard about lakes but never been to one,
                                                the

    as not the is or the it of it all we knew. Brother
  B spotted me the lake I knew best. There was Clear
    Lake a schoolmate told me about... No matter
  he spotted me it, this was not that lake. This wasn't
                                                one

of the places I'd have been I kept thinking, not
   a place called out at my Dogon funeral had I had
one. Here we were, somewhere else, Brother B my
   Virgilian escort, the not yet beloved lake all I knew

                                              to

   call it, Clear Lake though he said he'd let me say
it was… "There it is," he said, "Clear Lake." "I can't
see it," I said. "You've been rattled by bodily set-
back," Sister C chimed in, "that's why." There was a

                                        lake,

   though, I could see. I could see it wasn't Clear Lake.
   All clarity was gone, bottom stirred up the bounty
of light lost its way in, stare and go on staring though

                                              we

   did. What I saw was Bottom Lake. The binocular de-
vice I looked out from inside told me its name, Adam's
   eyes hijacked it seemed, a tale the flown ones told come

                                              true…

   We were the stolen ones, Brother B explained, the
   tol'you's toy, eyes at whatsay's mercy. A euphonious
   intimacy enticed us, he went on, the flown and the
lone ones gathered at the lake, the vicissitudes of going

                                        sewn

   into its rippling skin, bags of bones and water though
   we ourselves were. Each of us headed, Sister C took it

                                        up,

   toward what was now Lake Dispatch, the new name ham-
   mered into the lake's tendentious heaven, each inside the

                                              tenu-

   ous body we looked out
from

                        •

   Sister C grew more pensive the farther in we went,
      more and more the thinker she was, queen among the
learned, thought the alcove underness was. The lake

                                              lay

   calling for a concept. Brother B demanded a name
      not as yet found. The would-be body of water of lore
fell away as we looked for it, fell insofar as we looked

                                              for

   it, we who were to brook no looking… Air bloomed
      around what was known as the teller's imperative, each

of us taken in turn to be the teller, channeling the lake's
   portent. Lake the blank slate each of us wrote on, lake the
                                                            epi-
      tome scratch and scrape and stroke were, lake's first
   and furrowed almanac, all of which and more came thru…
      We recollected the Dread Lakes' dry bed, the figment of
   water we saw, Dread Lakes lore, less lake than legend, the
                                                            Dead

      Lakes rumor we saw… Sister C took her turn as teller. It
      was all, she said, transitivity's house, all an equation,
   Dread Lakes, Dead Lakes, Dead Locks. A matted mane the
                                                            re-
      gion wore, hearing her tell it, mane a mix of air and light.
   Brother B, taking his turn, said he couldn't see it, lake less
      image than thought, thought's play day, eponymous coif he
                                                            took

      it, eponymous coif no doubt, the clarity he'd have it have
   a clarity of concept, what the lake itself, he said, said it was or
      said it wanted. Clear Lake he again allowed we might call it…
   I wanted to pass. I wanted not to take my turn. Tell was too
                                                            pre-
      vious, Bottom Lake's legacy, call it Bottom Lake or Hear-
      say Lake, no matter, call it, as I was tempted to, Char Lake,
   Zvia's "Tell me true" taken to heart. I wanted not to cry, not
                                                            to
      scream, not to have tell coaxed out of me, the lake's puta-
   tive medium, moot squall. I spotted Sister C the studious
      one transitivity's house, a train of ises, is the lake's chain
                                                            of
   equations, the lake only lying there, is equaling is equaling is
                                                            e-
      qualing
   is

I spotted Sister C her conspicuous isness. I spotted
her her lakeside abidance, Brother B his deaconly "Take
your time." We stood on Skyline looking all the way

to

the ocean or we might as well have, the lake, we
felt, boundless now. Body of land, body of water, bod-
iliness broken between them. We might as well have
been on our way from La Honda, George Harrison on the

box,

1970, all things having to pass... Rafe and Karen might
as well have ridden with us, all things accruing to the rav-
enous time we knew them, broken again as we as well got

our

share

•

We were now calling ourselves the Long Since
   Chorale, Brother B and Sister C's chorus, Brother
B's latest last love song the song we sang. There
                                     was
   a we beyond we three, beyond those two, the
 we that looked on. Brother B lay headless, all arms,
   legs, torso. His head lay buried in musk… Broth-
er B let lake be look, the not yet beloved now beloved.
                                     He
   saw himself with his head up Sister C's dress. He
   saw himself nuzzle her behind. He saw himself study
crevice, contour, Sister C his paleolithic Venus, pear-
  bottom abundance, musky underness, musk upon musk,
                                  un-
   remitting remit… It seemed he'd been singing thru all
of time and we'd been singing, fanned by muni-bird wings,
  wing flutter, caroling ass-that-wasn't-glass, extolling butt,
                                 bot-
tom, bum. Song was his way of saying lake was likewise we
  sang, a last love song romancing love's discrepant lake,
  the lake not yet what it was. We stood lakeside a ways away
                                 from
   the lake, the long song's lengthening shadow… The lake
lay without gleam, neither glass nor glasslike, lay without glis-
  ten, a matte luminosity, nonce demur. It was all anything
                                but
clear but see-thru as well, a certain lake they were said to
   have circled, the thing that was its name, the thing its name
  said it was, we the migrating they the pas de deux that was,
                               Broth-
   er B and Sister C's
pirouette

We stood on the far side of sense, where sense
   turned in on itself, coexistent quality and qualm,
a contained ungainliness the lake was like. Sense
                                                   was
   the wick of a recumbent sun, blown out, black
      stub, black stick, black inveiglement, the bottom
of things, black trust… Bottom Lake was bottom-
   like, an opaque approximation, not so much lake as
                                                   like,
      we resided in doubt. We stood looking out on like.
   Lake was to like as was was to hearsay, gangliness the
                                                   order

      of the
   day

The lake, like everything else, was there but
not there, a tending-toward that was all we could
  hold. The same, Brother B said, went for Sister

                        C's
  bounty, musky recesses all there was of God
anymore, waft a kind of cocaine almost, waft
  coming off the beloved's thigh all there was of

                        wor-
  ship, obdurate, immaterial all the same… His lat-
  est last love song faded, back into the blue as unex-
  pectedly as it came out, a splay lake toccata played

                     on
  the small of Sister C's back, a tense, pretend in-
  tangible, tuck. Adoration's roundabout way verged
  on ornament, devotion to be spoken of as well…

                     A
self-nominated lake we saw reined itself up, ours
  to be taken, tawn lake. This the ride we were call-
ing desire, the lake the amenities of heaven, of all

                     that
  could occur an auspicious turn's coincident bid, its

                  or
another's transom sur-
mise

        •

The ride was only a wish not to be done, the lone
share we got of infinity, our impatience for which
  went on. We would forever be recollecting, circling

                     the
  lake, not knowing which lake it was or where, long
  on want. An ideal of equanimity it bodied forth
or lay embedded in, such as we had never seen, so late

                     we
  were, way late… We were back in *The Book of the*
Bug's Jaw, bites all over us, Sister C's meat-on-the-
  bone beauty no bulwark, the retreat Brother B made of

                     her
  no matter. A lake's worth of lotion it would've taken

to relieve us, the bug's jaw no joke. Infinite itch, to
hear the book tell it, the ride we pursued or we were put

up-

on by

OVERGHOST OURKESTRAL BRASS

—"mu" two hundred eleventh part—

We came to where tolls were to be paid,
allegorical it seemed, Piers Plowman and the
like had nothing on us. Love's wayward
                                        hand
      hugged our hips it could've been said.
    There was getting to be more of a rapport. We
    were God's trombones or God's trumpets,
                                        un-
clear which. We blew intervals that reenact-
    ed the Fall, so hollow we were, skid and
scree all bellow and bell. We were the Drop
                                        Choir,
      the Heartbreak Church again. We made it
make itself up out of strain, striving, subsist
    on extenuation, not a broken song no matter it
                                        sang
      breakage... We gave it a righteous, get-right
      sound, a reverend sound, heuristic horns feel-
ing out our prospects, heartbreak brass. We played
    pretty against playing pretty. To hear us was to
                                        be
      said goodbye to, to be told we were going,
    soon gone, to be privy to deathbed regrets. One
      sat bolt upright hearing it, yet another clime,
another clinic, suspect inside body under scrutiny,
                                        we
      blew unassured of our next breath. We were liv-
      ing inside but close to outdoors. Winged insects
crawled around inside our house, rummage our re-
    sources though we might or though we did, all that
                                        was
      ours at risk. We were imagining ourselves, pinch-
ing ourselves, not sure we were awake, the band we'd
    have been, pumped high, Heliopolis's pitch... But
                                        we
      were not a band or we were a band in mind only,
    the best kind Andreannette said, a pretend band,
      make-believe brass, an Aladdin's lamp we rubbed.
                                        We

blew as the box dictated. Something we were got-
ten to by was on the box, the box that would foliate
our book, be our book, a fine something we'd've one

                                      day

  learned to
 play

        •

Our way lay ahead, an open book. We had come
to the tolling place, allegorical it only seemed.
Toll was what bells did. We declared what we were

                              not

  saying, said again and again we were not saying
this or saying that, the chime of which rocked our
jaws, rang like sirens, an ocean of champagne to our

                              left,

  water with sun glint. We would work without look-
ing up we told ourselves, in but not of it, not Nub-
  bites, beautiful though the coast was, offshore brass
ventriloquial, offshore salting our throats… We were

                            farm-

  ing, eyes on the ground in front of us, brass bells had
  they been silver no distraction, our feet slapped at
by artichoke leaves. A low ride, a slow roll, had taken

                            us

  there, toll to be other than it was what took us, rub and
  reconnoiter the book we were enlarging, aleatory tap's

                              kis-

met

We were saying what we were not saying, not
saying what but by elimination. We were not Nub-
bites nor were we Nurians. Our whatsay said as
                                    much...
    In it but not of it, we knew too much. Sheaves
of wheat were bales of cotton were bundles of rods,
    a recessed choir caroling the wrong rule of the
world we brought brass against, would-be brass our
                                    dilu-
vian bequest. Birdseed cracked our teeth as we blew...
    Benedictory bells chimed faintly behind us. Crack-
ling blew, the horns' breakdown our thought piece, what
                                    there

    was of what there
    would be

We crackled. Crackling said say fell short, we
    crackled. Cracked birdseed stuck to our lips
that were now beaks, beaks that were suspect
                                    brass...
    In from offshore we crept, bugling taps, Lone
    Coast fog a shawl whose cover we moved under.
Parrots and parakeets, ibises and herons, a confer-
    ence of the birds crackling blueness, blown toll, the
                                    band's

        own emic
        bay

What set us going and was it going was
a curse was what we stood asking, foot-
  hills falling away to the west from where
                                        we
    stood, chill waters' namesake peace to
  be had we hoped, Magellan's misappellation
    made good. We stood on Highway 35, me
and Sophia. We had just gotten out of the car,
                                        the
    passenger door was open, "Acknowledge-
      ment" loud on the box. Trane's edge cut
  right thru us. We were both getting ready to
                                        be
    gone, a long leading up to it we hoped, if
      not, no matter, ready, if not, even so...
  "Our moment in the sun," Sophia said, and it
    was, a bright golden moment burnished by
                                        trum-
    pet and trombone, offshore brass we were
    never not aware was there. It was Lone Coast
    apprehended by Low Forest compass, life
  bound in looking out from Skyline, back to be
                                        reck-
    oned with sitting with Sophia near nightfall,
    brass tenuousness come nigh. Brass breakdown.
    Recollected lament. Eleanoir bid goodbye on
                                        the
    cliff at San Gregorio... All of life bound up in
      that she made it seem, lament's tranquility, the
  end or the beginning or both, she propounded,
                                        so
    much to be made of it, more than say-so she
    tallied, the hex of having come to be going,
      sheer lament reminiscing an ultimate where
  there was none. The foothills rolled away as
                                        we
    stood looking toward water we couldn't see,
      hex the very word off Sophia's tongue as we
  spoke of Eleanoir, the going and the being set
                                        go-

ing both. "Stalked," I owned up, "by my own
heartbeat," part paean, part complaint, copped
correlative gotten, gone, parallactic display or

                                        dis-

   patch… What was it gave going or being gone
such air, being sent such ardor we wondered, a
   kind of ember the pure gist of it we'd have said,
the closest we'd get to which was with Trane on

                                    the

   box and the offshore brass and the sun and the
   say-so, the subtlest wind in the world as we
stood there, the sky's blue bowl, the sky's one eye,
   the eye a lit flame, lit flame a struck match-head,

                                    ig-

nition so near, so far. Whatever it was, I was feel-
   ing it. Was it I saw what wasn't Sophia stood
   wondering out loud, was it I saw a would-be one,

                                    an

   Eleanoir that wasn't, Eleanoir's overghost. So, at
least, she said, said the offshore brass, matte sheen,
   matte shimmer, an invisible corolla, crown atop the

                                  head

   of the throneless, Queen She-of-the-Unshaved-
Legs… An arcade of redwood and eucalyptus far
   from Low Forest, deep ignition dictating still. What-
ever it was, I was feeling it. Trane's cauterizing cut it

                                 may-

be was, the day's expanse come to an edge or to a
   point, Trane's edge cutting right thru. Sunlight
as well cut thru, beams we thought back to streaming
   down in the redwood chapel, otherwise caught in

                                  the

   leaves or the needles, apostolic, striated light. I
was feeling it, whatever it was, the mere sound of her
   name talismanic. Something about the mounded-
ness of the earth, something about it rolling away. We

                                  see

more than we see Sophia was telling me, say some-
   thing back way beyond me no matter I tried, tongue
a dead weight in my mouth… There we stood on the

                                  side

   of the road and there we were it dawned on me, a
new-day apprehension under overghost Eleanoir's

tutelage, offshore brass a bereft hustle. Having's not
                                                    hav-
     ing gave a sway to the way she walked, to bask in
   whose auspice was all one could want, no less than
     that what we meant by the going, slapped on our be-
   hinds at birth. Sophia grinned, an admission she got
                                                    that
     I got it, glint as off an edge of broken glass. We'd be
     forever mulling it over, savoring the conceit were
   that what it was, forever pondering it I could see, the
                                              slap
     we spoke of without speaking, the behind of which
     we also spoke, the goad that went with us in walking…
     The diffuseness of it was maybe what it was, what I
                                                    was
     feeling, the something I was feeling, the sting of
   that walk and recalling that walk, Trane in the air and
     the sun and the say-so, Sophia and the offshore brass.
   Whatever it was, I was feeling it, had at by the ground
                                                    and
       by the air and by memory, had at by Sophia's ensor-
       cellment, psychic rasp and arrest. The ground we
   stood on had grown sacred, ground I could imagine
     Eleanoir might have walked on, held between whose
                                              raspy
     legs I dreamt myself, my own legs brushed by hers.
     Or was it all ground had grown sacred or potentially
     was I wondered. Sophia, reading my mind it seemed,
                                              asked
       outright. Was it the nature of ground, the nature of
   standing, she stood asking, once one let it dawn on one,
     once one gave it a chance… "Chance's ghost," I let
                                        out,
   tongue suddenly free of its weight, as if all were exact-
     ly that, that itself but a trace of itself, a probabilistic
   pitch that might or might not have been, ground as much
                                                    open-
     ing as cover, no lasting stand to be had as yet. "Psycho-
       geomancy," I said, "let's call it." "Best to be above
   it," she said, the earth at our feet inconsolate, we as well
                                                    from
       head to toe, Eleanoir's and my youth at the time now
       a taunt. We cocked our ears toward the offshore brass, a

silent world of sememe, sign, ythmicity. "Horns don't go
there," she said, making it up I thought. As was I possibly

I

thought but I was feeling it. Whatever it was, I was feel-
ing it. It was all so inordinate I thought, whatever it was,
the horns we couldn't hear, the water we couldn't see, a

se-

cret world whose effects we moved at large in, an im-
manence unvalved, unstopped... We cocked our heads and
we cupped a hand behind an ear, the airiness of all as-
sumption evident, whatever it was made of moment by my

fail-

ing lungs, my failing legs. Imminent or eventual depar-
ture gave it something it got. Whatever it was, I was
feeling it. It felt good to've gotten out of the car, out into the
allness it was, what Sophia called allness, out of the car's

com-

paction and into it. Where horns don't go we gave more
thought, haptic abeyance the notion we floated. Sophia
taunted me with the thought of Eleanoir, intimated a wad

of

dark hair inside the crotch of her white panties, there that
horns would or would want but won't, a closed world of
touch and remote admission. "Brazen," Sophia said, "a

joke,

'reinforced crotch' as they say." The close world of bodily
crevice loomed, all outdoors no matter, the close world of
bodily musk two-ply cotton was the harbinger of. All of it

was

only a launch, offshore so abstract brass itself pervaded
the air. Rare haze, rare wick, split ignition... Waft and
resplendence were afoot, the mere thought of which was

to

be set going, as if all outdoors came down to a crux, an un-
derness, a glimpse of which was whose forfeiture, the going
and the being gone whose chase we were. Sophia saw that I

saw

and she grinned, offshore brass grown immense with in-
audibility, brass tint a kind of almost touch. Shimmer
had to do with it, as did shadow. To think was to blow leg-
bone flute, tint contour, nuzzle faint recesses as one blew.

"The

fleetingness of the world must've was what I was after,"

I told Sophia, accent on "must've was." Whatever it was,
I felt it, breath a bead of heat on the flute's opening, faint

legs'

recompense. Whatever it was, I was feeling it, waft and re-
monstrant wick, stray redolence, the at-large-ness of some-
thing so recessed it grew revenant, legbone embouchure's

tac-

tile strafe... All it was was we stood looking toward La
Honda, toward Half Moon Bay. To think was to be as we
were. To think was to've been there and gone, reminiscent
remit, the unseized impeachable truth of it, ever the trace.

To

think was to blow wind into the wind, ever the wisp, ever
aware what we carried where our legs met, not to be alone with
whose aromas what love was, the getting, the going, foothill,

for-

est, buttock, the at-large absorption of things. To think was
to be in brass territory, no matter one played a legbone flute. We
were going backwards trying to catch up, not catching up. I

ima-

gined all the life I couldn't see, marmots in the woods in
Canada and such. I said as much to Sophia, recollecting sunset
light on Eleanoir's face aeons before in Big Basin, Lone Coast
before it became Lone Coast, something seen in a face no face

could

avail one of. Toss was all it was, waft redolence's release...
I went to go on but Sophia said, "Hush now, don't." Horns do
go there I thought, offshore brass nowhere if not, the where that
was and, whatever it was, wasn't, whatever it was, what I was

feel-

ing, feeling's inordinacy. A chubby butterfly flew by, my funny
valentine I thought, nothing if not Sophia, the way she looked at
that moment, plump of wrist and of ankle I noticed, not the first

time.

Whatever it was, whatever I saw, I was feeling it, Sophia's tu-
telary presence were that what it was, her light cotton dress down
past her calves, her light-bodied bigness, totemic fly-by. It was

as

much her big-bodied lightness I thought, silhouetted legs the
near side of the sun. To think was to be fed an affection for in-
definiteness blur fostered, limbs under loose-fitting cloth pen-
tecostal fret, protruding lower leg, ankle and foot sheer wick, hiero-
glyph if not... To think was to orient oneself, position oneself,

noth-

ing if not what Sophia did, standing on the tips of her toes as if
in pointe shoes, right hand up at her brow shading her eyes, the
   brim of a cap the top of her head might've been, light-bodied big-
ness, big-bodied lightness or both. I stood noticing the amplitude

                                                                    she
garnered, she of the sunlit cotton, she of the "Hush now" counsel,
   Trane's ode accreting coming out of the car. To think was to reach
with the calipers of heaven, as was not to, one to be told from the

                                                                    oth-
   er by pitch or inflection. We stood not knowing what degree
      west we were, what degree north. We reflected on the going or
the getting, the getting going, all the dense, dusty redwood green

                                                                    fall-
   ing away to the west. Sophia remained on her toes, hand on her
   brow like a visor. She said, "Notice how it spreads or how, hav-
ing spread, it sits. Notice the at-large-ness of it, heaven's moot
largesse," hers no voice if not the stranded voice of heaven, none if

                                                                    not
   at-large-ness's own. Trane's voice, strained and stranded, infil-
      trated hers. Her strong toes, her strong calves and her strong an-
kles had her standing tall, stranded heaven's collectedness put to

                                                                    the
   test… It was just as Ogotemmêli had said. Someone like a wom-
      an wearing a woman's dress had come down from heaven. She
      stood on her tiptoes as if trying to return, large body lifted into

                                                                    hea-
   ven were her way to be had, light body heavenly I thought. Her
      anklet, her earrings and her necklace were no one's bones though,
thin adornment all the more of the going, getting, heavenly mind's

                                                                    au-
   ric demand. To think was to see it so. What degree west we were
      was of no import nor was what degree north. No matter what it
was, whatever it was, I was feeling it, waywardness and weight, wheth-
er at odds or in cahoots. I was thinking Alan Silva was right, I knew

                                                                    what
   "celestrial" meant. Something so not there was there I was think-
ing, blank pages The Book of So's appendices. Horns, no matter how
   ably played, don't go there I was thinking, the sophic degree, the
sophic factor, a kiss that had been a long time coming called arrivancy,

                                                                    the
   womanly degree Sophia made it seem, the womanly factor… I was
thinking what Santana said about sugarcane was right. I was getting the
last bit of sweetness out, the long goodbye it all was or would turn

                                                                    out

to've been, love's maculate precincts, made light of though they
were. We had pulled over on our way back from the rickety hospi-
   tal. We stood looking down at the woods, no marmots there though
                                                                        I
thought them or maybe there were, Sophia's tiptoe lift a momentary
   inspiration I hadn't seen before, pudgy wrists and feet an unexpect-
   ed boon, Trane woven into it all saying horns don't go there. I felt
                                                                      al-
   most dead, free of the future. Whatever it was, I was feeling it, not
                                                                    feel-
   ing my legs, my
lungs

INSOFAR-I'S AT-LARGE ADDRESS

—"mu" two hundred thirteenth part—

When I looked inside myself it loomed
    outward, when I searched outside it
stole back in. But what I said would be
                                sing-
    ing sang, the turn between in and out,
out and in, the lilt up or down that was
    both for a moment, lush work not of the
                                turn
        but of turning, Eulipion condolence I
    consoled myself with... Not since before
    I lay busted up had I not lain busted up,
the hard work of waking again. I was one of
                                the
    lucky ones. They cut a hole in my leg and
they sewed it up. All balance, were there to be
    balance, would gather against the wall brass
                                was,
        offshore debridement and bray. Brass was
    a wall of thought, thought circumambient
    wood, looks given back it got and filled up
                                with...
    Brass gave and it took away, the day's run a
        reflection tossed aside. I knew nothing if not
brass but I knew nothing, the taste it left on
                                my
        teeth a run of zinc. A certain something
    prevailed, a certain strain I was prone to be-
        come obsessed with. Brass was all I knew. A
holding forth no one would've called singing
                                bore
    down on us, the ugliness of Nub no joke, Nub,
        Nublicans, no joke. I was one of the lucky
    ones. They took pictures and then they cut... It
                                was
    all I could do not to laugh. Salt burned away
        what was left of my stomach, in my belly the
beast whose belly I was in. All the doctors were
    Nublicans, the surgeons were all generals, having
                                noth-

ing but the cut was no joke. I stood in thought's
capital, near but not laughing. Brass bore the import
of thought without allowing it, bore it, all anyone

                                                             could
    without cracking, like laughter, short of collapse...
    Brass had grown ominous. It felt funny feeling
lucky to be cut. Nublicans in lab coats attended me,

                                                         no
easy take on who they were, said, as they were, to
    be winning, to be on top... From what I could tell,
    they were a kind of cop, one's convalescence

                                                     bro-
ken in on by them or by the world, one's now
foreign body broken in. Brother B said it appeared
to be Rum's Free Hospice. I told him he was a

                                                  blip,
go away... I'd broken a law getting sick but I was
    one of the lucky ones. The surgeons burned where
    they couldn't cut but I was lucky, completely cut

                                               a-
way

           •

Hospital gowns were falling from the sky, more
    plentiful than ever. Rooms and beds were falling
too. They knocked us down as we caught them,

                                               legs
    failing. They were calling it curbside, they were
calling it concierge, calling it everything but con-
valesce. Brother B said I'd been on trial but I slept

                                           thru
    it. They were calling it cubicle, they were call-
ing it corner office. Some called it Nub, some called
it Nur... Before I lay busted up I lay busted up.
Busted up was the way I came in, the way I'd go out,

                                        noth-
ing if not the me of me I heard it announced. To be
me was to be that way. Busted up was what to be me
was. It was my fault. All our knives arrayed and sorted,

                                        I
    was going outside going inside, Mr. Neither One,
    Mr. In-Between. It wasn't, I reminded myself, my

fault or it wasn't, someone else reminded me, my
                                        fault,
    Brother B maybe… I kept catching the inside of
my lip between my incisors, I kept chomping the in-
    side of my cheek, the beast whose belly I was in
come up out of mine. My body was no longer mine or
                                        had

    never
been

Nonslip socks fell from heaven in the recension
I read, the book of the body's breakdown Nub would
  have none of, the book of the body's breakdown

                                        legion,
     no bible not at base that book. Nub had moved
  on, turned itself into myth, it was said, the land
  of everlasting youth… The return of the book was
a kind of reflux. I slept on a cot so thin I lay on my

                                        side.
     I sang the beloved's body still, busted up no matter,
        gnostic bait some warned it was no matter, new-
  ly of the school of the Anuncians, I sang the beloved

                                        bod-

     y's deeper sleep inside
my sleep

•

I had a sense of others in my vicinity loitering,
  passing thru, each as though vignette were
enough, tableau were enough, a wisp or a shear
                            mi-

  rage otherwise. A young woman pushed a ba-
by stroller. An adolescent boy hawked athletic
  wear. They moved animated by thought appar-
ently other than their own, the composite mind
                            they'd

  have claimed habitude to be, a music they'd
  have gone so far as to say, composite music,
figures caught in passing, flashers, no doubt in
  my mind they were there… I held my fist in my
                            hand,

  a piece of wood. I dozed off, as was the corner
office's wont. I lay with both fists balled up by
  the time I started awake, each a piece of wood
                            with

  brass between its fingers, custom fit for Rum,
Nub, Nur. I wanted to say I'd had my fill, I'd
  had my say for a while, but it wasn't true. I still
kept catching the inside of my lip between my
                          in-

  cisors. I kept chewing the inside of my cheek,
  the beast in my belly in my mouth. Combinatory
law drew me on but this wasn't that, not so it as
                          that,

  its it of it long since collapsed on itself. The
metaphysics of the blip was what it was, what it
  there was, the catch of glass at the eye's cor-
ner lost and gone watery, blur's claim on blip the
                          new

  page not yet written, seen's claim on say… I
went on, sooth said in a hospital gown had it ever
  been said, the beast my mouth biting itself was
                          was

a kind of talk, Nub's eventual book of the people,
  Popul Vuh. My bites narrated our obscurity, want-
ing to or not, sooth said, had sooth ever been said,
                          by

  the damage it
was

•

I was in a hospital gown but no hospital,
   curbside service the name it went by, one
of the names it went by. I kept imagining
                                        mas-
      tery, only to find it fell apart. I lay chas-
   ing it, dreamt I lay chasing it, never to be
      caught short or caught out I promised my-
self, only to find it fell apart. I shivered and
                                        shook,
      embarrassed, outside under a sheet so thin.
   I went under the knife dancing limbo I want-
ed to say or did in fact say, wanting it to be
                                        true...
      Doctor D I kept calling myself, Sister C's
         prodigy, Brother B's brother, the man with
a plan, at last. I went out joking with one of
                                        the
      nurses, a quip about "affable care" the last
   crack I remember. I went under laughing at
      affable's play on *affordable*, Nub's non-truck
                                        with
      either. Curbside, boutique, concierge, cor-
   ner office, drive-by, all of a piece... And then
      this as I went under, from which to which
                                        clime
      or clinic I couldn't say: *I remained of the be-*
      loved's brigade no matter I lay busted up,
no matter the gown I wore, the beloved's limbs
                                        and
      midriff a dream of deliverance, a dream of
      extravagance, amorous care she nor I could
                                        af-
ford

_____

Had I gotten well or were they kicking me out
    I wondered. Nub had moved into myth, it
was said, and we all followed, compensative

                                           yarn
    putting us inside and out, complicit certain
ways of looking called it. Fair enough, I thought.
Too easily, I thought... My gown opened in

                                        back,
     meaning something. My gown had come
down from the sky, meaning something. Mean-
ing set things in relief, as did myth. My gown

                                      rose
    off me and caught fire, rose into the blackest sky
     there'd ever been, consumed as it rose, launch-
ing sparks as it burned, sparks that became what we

                                         call

   stars

The sky was a cloth whose colors ran, we
   moved on, bone-deep abidance come
with us, at the crux what could not but be
                        re-
peated we found out. A kind of high scat
kept at us, a not-to-be-said something said
   or insisted again and again, moved with or
                       with-
   out, moving or not... Clumps of rope in
our gullets were hard to digest but we digest-
ed them, no not knowing what history was.
                        It
was all so abstract and at the same time right
   in our faces, all of it going on leaving more to
go on. Abstract finding concrete was no joke. I
                     sat
   at the back of the bus, body language say-
ing exactly that, the way I slumped... The qui-
   eter it got the more mixed our feelings were,
                     the
more mixed our feelings the quieter it got. The
   day lay like a slab inside us. What to do and
what to say had at us, high scat a kind of question
                     we
   were put upon by, what no more the crux of
    them than how, how portended, crux brought
to bear on us repeatedly, at us as the is or the it
   of it, was's day redone... We were in the hands
                     of
   the Nublicans, no such thing as enough. We
kept the news on, ready for the next outrage. The
   sky whose colors ran was an allegorized polis
whose colors were us, remain where we were and
                     as
we were though we tried to no matter. We kept
   returning to the news, asking, "Are we dead yet?"
We all but were, not knowing what, not knowing
                     how,
   high scat's entou-
rage

•

Insofar-I's homeopathic hum stayed with us,
   a slap to the head ever the tonic. We each were
Dr. D with exactly the answer, Patient P as well,
                      hedg-

   ing our bets. We wore gowns open as books but
open in back, recondite address in reserve they
   seemed to say. Ever the back and forth, ever the
                     dia-

   lectic we could wish. We set out reminiscing
Nub's facelift, we who long knew it had claws…
   Otherwise we were helpless, me the most I
thought. Each of us maybe thought that way, he
                     or

   she the most. We all, no matter where we sat,
sat in back. We wanted to be lost in the stars, astral
   black. It wasn't just the creaking of the word we
                   heard

   or it was but the word included more than we
knew. We wanted to be lost and found and brought
   back big-eyed, see our way thru, rhyme a kind
                  of

creaking in *The Book of So*… It might have been
   Neptune the bus was crossing for all I knew. I
gazed inward, not out, slouched on the backseat so
                  low

   I couldn't see. "At the crux what's crucial," I was
repeating, a low oath or a kind of adage I steadied
   myself with. It might have been the Bay Bridge the
                  bus

   was crossing for all I knew, the dunes of the Go-
bi Desert for all I knew. All I knew was we flew
   thru the dark behind my eyelids, late of the ump-
teenth clinic or clime, an ambulance we might as well
                  have

   been in. Ahdja picked up "At the crux what's crucial"
   and intoned it with me, wrack mantra more and
more the longer it went on, mystic beast about on pad
                  and

   claw, thick Vedic
   moan

•

"At the crux what's crucial" was an all but ade-
noidal burr, high scat's midmost reach. High scat
itself said otherwise, the backs of our clothing
                                        torn.
    Said what it said and said otherwise, word
from all sides at once. The inner me threw my
hands up. On a CT screen I'd seen a white dot
                                        that
kills, on a TV screen the baby prez's war rattle.
    As without, so within, I lay low thinking… I lay
dreaming I lay nuzzling Ahdja's back and buttocks,
                                        Ah-
dja my mantric accomplice, her heavenly back-
sides what respite there was. I sat slouched at the
back of the bus, ever the hound, nuzzling the musks
                                        of
heaven. Another clime, another clinic. Another
lurch, another going forth… How it got to be about
me made me wonder, it-being-about the targeted
                                        sense
each of us dreaded, better to look on from outside.
    It-being-about made one the it of it removed,
the hollowness it ultimately was one's own, enacted
execution style. This was my meditation on death,
                                        Hol-
low House, death's edifice the back of the bus I
sat slouched in, ever there to be picked off I thought.
    Some said social, some somatic, I said both. All it was
was a holding tank I thought, the it of all its, doled-out
                                        ex-
cursion even so, death's ration… We bumped along,
    moving on, *Hollow House Excursus* the book we
thumbed and were in, volume number none of us knew
                                        of
The Book of So, inside and outside both. As without, so
    within, I reminded myself, wanting to bury my head
away from it all but unable to, Ahdja's "At the crux what's
                                        cru-
cial" intertwined with
mine

•

(chant)

There was a box in the bus, Billy Harper was on
   the box. His hard squall cut my head off, the bur-
  ial I'd been hoping for. The picture of a journey
                              lin-

gered on in my severed head. We had come to
a hill I felt, another clime, another climb. We were
  climbing when something gave out, bordered on
                               sub-

  limity but quit… It was beginning to say good-
bye, saying let it be a long goodbye, greasing the
   wheels of quantity I felt or I thought, could my bur-
ied head be said to've thought. None of it related but
                               by

  recoil to Nub's rolled head, a stream of Tiki torch-
  es' would-be turning back of time. I was climbing
stairs in the lingering picture my head was when my
  foot went out from under me, slipped on a step rain
                              had

  fallen on, entropy and accident's tryst. I lay scratch-
ing my head, slouched in the backseat scratching my
  head, the back of the bus the chalkboard my head had
                              be-

  come, vèvès told me tell my horse… The back of
the bus was all chalk inscription, a thin wall between
  in and outside, a kind of sheetrock. The way the two
                              par-

took of each other was on the one side Hollow House
  Local, the other Hollow House Express. I sat slouched,
breathing in and out, each breath a bead I thumbed, there
                              was

  a rash all over my chest. As within, so without, I la-
mented, Charlottesville, Barcelona, gnostic body one was
  born into unawares, not knowing, known as it broke it-
self down… Body politic. Body impolite. Talk of cells
                              no

  matter which. Cells' apparent containment only ap-
parent. Gnostic membrane. Would-be husk. These as
  well were beads I thumbed. Outline. Inside. Concept.
                              Con-

sonant. Boll. Burble. Bust. Insofar-I's hum was back had
it ever left, "Are we dead yet?" a kind of collateral, the
sky's run of color's low lingering cloth... The sky's run of
col-
or come nigh, the bus rolled on. The remote place my
head lay buried in propelled it, an advancing notion of
love despite it all. *The rash gets redder and won't go away,*
I wrote in my notebook, not meaning to be symbolic but
no-
ticing maybe it was. At Nub's helm the open sore that
had taken soul's place no matter, the bus rolled on, we
were climbing the stars. *I was climbing the stairs when a
bone broke,* I wrote. Burial grounds underlay my house in
hea-
ven. *Written,* I wrote, *ridden. It was something I wrote,
something I rode, love social and semantic were what it was
love, love and hate, a hard line between...* The bus rolled
on.
Billy kept at it on the box, an astrolabe it might have
been. Like unto like, time abreast itself, the hole my head
was tossed into, the hole otherwise in my head. A two-
headed Dr. D I might've been, a two-headed Patient P. *Love
so-
cial and somatic,* I wrote, crossed out what I wrote before.
Crossed out *somatic,* rewrote *semantic,* Mr. Back-and-
Forth, crossed out *semantic,* rewrote *somatic,* crossed out *so-
matic,* rewrote *semantic,* ever the dialectic I wrote wishing,
ever
the back and forth... Ahdja thought of it as crux and cruciality.
She looked over my shoulder as I wrote, we went on roll-
ing, we were climbing the sky. The back of the bus became a
kind
of notebook, the chalkboard gave way to ballpoint and pen-
cil, ink vévé, lead vévé. We were climbing the stars when our
clutch broke, climbing the stars when my foot slipped and my
hip
gave out, climbing the stars when the pen went dry, climb-
ing the stars when the pencil broke, Billy Harper on the box
all the while. It was a box inside a box given what the bus had
be-
come, a remote pit my head lay buried in what my head had be-
come... Crux and cruciality a box inside a box. Entropy and ac-
cident, crux and what counted, song, like any other, every other,
long

since, song forty-seven times
five

Gnostic body one was born into not knowing, rude or
  politic, gross or of ether, social body, subtle, the same.
Hard not to see congruence, dark brought out to light,
                                                      the
  closer walk with gloom one was taking, whether one
  walked or not… High scat spoke into the pit my head lay
  in, a remote promise reneged on made again it seemed.
                                                  We
  will have had time, it seemed it said, to rest our chins
  on the heels of our hands and reflect. One was begin-
    ning to feel almost gone, used up, not with long to stay.
                                            Born
  beginning to say goodbye, one said it louder now, the open
  sore that had taken soul's place at Nub's helm, the comb-over's
                                              hav-
  oc fix, as well begun to say
goodbye

III
PHLEGM

SEVEN EAST IMPROMPTU

—"mu" two hundred fifteenth part—

So they wheeled me out, the Sick Man of Ool-
   Ya-Koo. They stood me up, I was one of
them now, we were a band. We stood inside
                                   au-
   diting out, nowhere the eye might light for
solace. At times we were a band in that we
   made music, only in that we hung together at
                                   oth-
er times, ginned-up harassment rubbing who's
out in, Nub's new look nastier by the day. We
   stood inside auditing out, a picture language on
the public terrain clear as ice… We leaned in as
                                 ever
   and as never before, the Elegiac String Extet
we'd have had it, non-bow held at the ready with
non-violin, non-viola, non-cello, non-bass, the
                               non-
   strings chanting no time lost. "We can't be
coming in here busting you up you say but we
can," I'd've sworn I heard them say, nonso-
nance's way they worked without peer. I knew it
                               was
   about Nub no matter what, nowhere the eye might
   light for solace. I knew my night mind's black
prognosis, Nub in deep league with my disrepair,
                              the
   Sick Man of Oo-Bla-Dee… I wrinkled my lips
   to whistle, no whistle. I lip-synched "You're
Still A Young Man." If we could just get a chorus
   going, I kept thinking, find a line that would lie
                              like
   a kind of net underneath it all, sung warily again
and again, caution but also cushion, if we could just get
   that, I was thinking, all would be well. All would not
                              be
   well I knew as I thought it, nothing get us out from
   under the wound inflicted on us, tacking like rickety
caravels as we did, wooden ships back in the day. An
                            ellip-

tical chorus ensued, hard not to tear up being joined
by it I found, wanting to squeeze, wanting to get and be
  got next to… Wanting to be thought beautiful I stood
                                                    bust-
ed up, all but choked on my own tongue, my medicinal
  stomach, medicinal jaw, the Sick Man of Omnibus
  Oo. An environmental croon it came to be, the chorus's
                                                    ad-
    ditive address. A blanket of shadow kisses lighting
down it sounded like, thick as butterflies on Lone Coast.
  Goddesses come from close to the sun it sounded like,
hot consorts we were told would wear us out, those of
                                                    us
  of the moon, the moon a drop of semen some said.
    All of it went to say, it wanted to say, it sounded like
  nothing, so meta my instinct was to duck or to hit the
                                                    floor
    but I went on standing, phlegm forever caught in my
  throat… An environmental cringe it came to be, whatever
  flora, whatever fauna there was withdrew, the Omnibus
                                                    Oo
    whose infirmary it was I stood up in. A band around
  my wrist told me my name and my birthdate. The color of
                                                    my
    socks meant I might
  fall

The changes came at me fast. Some of the names
　　were not the same. Insofar-I was Mine-I, I-Insofar
　　was O'ai. I crossed my heart, said hope to die. I
　　　　　　　　　　　　　　　　　　　　　　stood
with the weight of boots on my feet, I stood unshod
in yellow socks no matter. I lip-synched "Under the
Boardwalk." I put a pill mouth on mercury, alchemy's
　　　　　　　　　　　　　　　　　　　　　　　best...
　　Medicine coated my tongue, no mead of the bards
of yore, no such mead as I'd read about, spit what
　　had been nectar, powder what had been pill. I stood
　　　　　　　　　　　　　　　　　　　　　　with
long Osirian feet that looked like only one foot, one leg,
　　one foot. I stood sideways, looked at from the side, it ap-
peared, mercury so admirably made I drew two life spans
　　　　　　　　　　　　　　　　　　　　　from

one

(29.viii.17: for alice coltrane)

I stood with Oosirian feet I meant to say, the Sick
Man of Omnibus Oo. Oosirian feet that looked like
only one foot I meant to say, one leg, one foot, in the
style
of *The Book of the Dead*... I had been reading about
when third legs jetted mercury, an alchemical body, as
I wished for a longer life. I could feel it being cooked by
this or that austerity, an Egypto-Vedic insistence upon
the
one

WANTING TO BE ABOUT ALCHEMY BUT NOT

—"mu" two hundred sixteenth part—

"Beyond a certain point," Tête could be heard say-
  ing, one of the consorts from close to the sun,
studious Tête, small-breasted Tête, Tête short for
                                          pe-
  tite. I heard myself snore, I'd fallen asleep. I
growled at myself, snorted, snapped. "Sweet con-
  cord," Tête continued, "subsides," the same
                                          as
  I was thinking. No time soon, I was thinking,
    would it linger among us, soon come though we
  promised ourselves. Chorus, amen corner, call us
                                          what
    one would, sweet accord we sang, soothing our-
      selves. No time soon would we give up, end
  our talk, no polite stutter, no not telling, no one
                                          want-
    ing to know what soul was. Sweet accord. Sub-
  liminal cherry. The sibilance of *someday soon*...
  Tête with her black-rimmed glasses, scholarly Tête
I couldn't take my eyes off. Something seen in a face
                                          no
  face could answer for. "The inconsequence of bod-
    ily life," I went to say but held back, "facial remit's
  disconnect." We were climbing a hill it seemed, we
                                          were
  circling a lake, circling a fountain. Coins had been
    tossed it was clear. I was playing the mystic or had
    gone to but drawn back, that a draft mix we might
                                          drink
  or a draft waft we might catch, I put powder under my
    tongue. Tête played wary sojourner, cinnabar long
given up on. She said honey and lemon might do just as
  well, cinnabar and honey mixed with lemon the recipe of
                                          yore
    I once made up she meant me to recall... I'd written it
  making light of her reading the *Treatise on the Dragon
  and the Tiger* she reminded me. It was a long time ago
                                          but

she remembered, back in the day or in another life
maybe, done for in that world but for the eked-out elixir
she sipped. It was a very long time ago but I as well

                                                    re-
membered. The air was a sphere companionate faces
    looked in and out from, the we of much mention, Tête's
the most prominent after what "Beyond a certain point"

                                                    set
    off. She was one of the sun's consorts my body re-
treated from, an alchemical hoax or an alchemical cure
    it all carried back to, bodies whose places waft and
remission took… It was what it was, no rendering the we

                                                    of
    much mention, the one of much mention, each a means
        of leverage, abstract. Tête stood observing her waist and
legs. "I avow the faultiness of the body," she said, gravi-
tating toward ghosthood. There was a hard way about her,

                                                    as
    about me, no quick majesty would either of us buy. It
        was maybe time for us to grow weary… We were pure
huddle, hubbub. "We're who we have," Tête said, part

                                                    con-
dolence, part caveat. Even so, I could only stare into
space or look at her face and say nothing, something seen
    in a face ever the riddle it was. Sipped, eked-out elixir

                                                    was
    the glimpse one got or the gaze one gathered, the lips
and the eyes of the philosophers one heard it said, the body

                                                    parts
    of God one heard it
said

It was what it was, no rendering otherwise, the we of
 much mention, the one of much mention, each a means
of leverage, abstract. Tête stood observing her waist and
                legs.
 "I avow the faultiness of the body," she said, gravitat-
ing toward ghosthood. There was a hard way about her, as
 about me, no quick majesty would either of us buy. It
                was
  maybe time for us to grow weary... Hadn't we had
 enough, suffered enough, we were asking, wasn't it
 clear to the eye we were no threat, evident for all to see
it was otherwise, obvious to the eye who the predators
              were,
 who pursued whom. All of it fell on deaf ears, those of
            Nub's

 not-see re-
solve

•

Tête had a hard way about her, as did I, some-
thing seen in a face neither facial remit nor re-
mand, one found oneself lost in thought. Tête
                                        fad-
    ed as the way moved on, uppercase "w" I'd
have thought but hesitated, decided not. Tête
herself promoted uppercase before being gone,
                                        fad-
ed as the Way moved on… I longed for what the
    book, were there a book, would avow, what there
being a book would avow. There had been a book
                                        said
    to preserve the wet of kisses, be where kisses
kept, a book that could once be seen but was now
    invisible, the book on which all subsequent
books were based. A recursive book it turned out
                                        to
    be for a moment, no sooner said to have been
        than it was back, the book of the moment's full-
ness could it be caught… It could not be caught
                                        but
    I could feel it, as if longing made it so, Tête's or
any other leave-taking the "long since" what balm
there'd be would issue from. I remembered I knew
                                        the
    book and that I knew more than could come from
books. Pine bark went from green to gold outside
    our vehicle. The more I looked the more wood went
lapis, the stone the philosophers taught accrues to all
                                        na-
    ture… The book was my friend but no longer need-
    ed, the alchemico-yogic body it promised faded
like Tête had. We were chemo sapiens now, we had
                                        che-
    mo, alchemico-anything gone. Were clinics climes
or had they taken climes' place this led us to won-
der, no longer with names like "Gift of Indra," "One
                                        Jew-
el," "Portion," "Skilled." By now one's head was the
    other side of a wall called Yonder, thought's un-
thinkable outside. All I wanted, no matter wanting
                                        fore-

closed it, was to be without appetite, all enjoyment...
Was that what they meant by gold I wondered, was it
that they were getting at with elixir I wondered, went

on

wishing I
knew

Wishing I knew was my ballad whim, a kind of
   willfulness, a stiffening lotus petal, a lifted edge.
It went on longer than it needed to Tête said, back

                                       in
   the picture now, went on with no need at all I'd
   already thought... I was reading a book about Tantric
   books, reading against the book Nub threw. I dozed

                                       off
   on every page of the book thrown at me, Nub's
   eternal defendant it seemed... We were back in the
   Stick City Ashram but not quite, my yogic body

                                 man-
qué. Fish Belly, Moon Island, Mare's Mouth and all

                                  attest-
   ed andoumboulou-
ousness

All the books, Insofar-I noticed, were written in
  verse, the elsewhere poetry was was the one
alchemy, the elsewhere music was, held to what
                                    held
    him steady, shake him as much as it might...
Glenn's double trio was on the box, "Thinking of
  Frank" echoed Frank homaging Trane. All was
                                  wist,
    a certain sadness, reprise. Insofar as it was a
band I blew, whether or not I blew, no need to make
  more of it than that. Breath caught inside a bub-
ble in my throat bore my colloquist wish... Not one
                                death
    but many, as had been said, the apprehension of it
a kind of death itself, each apprehension. Insofar-I was
                              count-
   ing, as was I, losing
count

Next we came to the Giblet Rim Split, epic
fragment. Not since Amma's clavicle spill-
  age had we seen so much debris, all the omen

                said

    to've been said by the wind strewn all over.
Burst wholeness's freedom fight it appeared
  all of, nothing less, burst wholeness's eternal

                drift.

  "Bodily breakdown, be my ledge, my light," we
  each intoned, a prayer long handed down among
our tribe... We sauntered in waltz time as past a

              flash-

  point, muffled albeit it was, in what was Nub,
what was Nur, what was Crater, knees and hips
  listing it seemed. Sway Head we each were calling

             our-

  selves, querulous eyebrows afoot. The news had had
  us up early and up late, wondering what outrage was
next. We needed our heads to be blown into we felt,

             we

  felt our heads needed to float, fill with Toulali's
  out-of-breath voice. One needed one's own voice to
  go colloquy, go nightingale, go sparrow, go hoopoe.
One's nod needed an answering chorus, one's voice

             to

  go weak as they shored it up. One felt one's voice
    needed to go partridge, go swan, go owl, go thirty...
All this on a mute surface we scratched as we made

            our

  way farther. The Rim Split had a riblike look to it,
    a wishbone look by turns. Clavicle spill recalled our
dinosaur roots, the birds we momentarily were or we

            felt

  we needed to be. Rim Split augured a tight squeeze,
  Crater's reptilian claw, Crater's brain the size of an
  almond. Sophia wept it so ailed us, testament, what
solace there was, no solace. She walked inconsolate,

            as

  did we all, Nub's unlikely pass where giblet met rib,
  sway heads aplenty though we were or that we were,

dance a condolence of sorts our legs approached. But
                                                    be-
    yond lay less desolate terrain we told ourselves. We
    were dreaming Nub went back to its facelift, we were
    dreaming the comb-over's jowls went away. Roses
    opened outside Toulali's lips and made it so or made it
                                                    ap-
    pear so. We kept time atop a bed of strings and horse-
    tail hair, clapped keeping time as we walked… The no-
    where music was grew closer as we made our way, was
                                                    our
    way, what but it would get us anywhere we thought. The
    elsewhere it also was drew nigh, noise Nub grew synony-
    mous with its other. "The Giblet Rim Split," we all said
                                                    at
    once as if to rescind it, sighed as we said it, remiss. We
    were juggling nowhere, anywhere, everywhere and
    elsewhere, name no dominion, noise not to be bound by,
                                                    as-
    sonant no matter it was. We let the as-if of it bear us a-
    long, the nowhere elsewhere was a new boon Toulali's
    roses brought news of, stop-time isthmus we knew as of
                                                    old,
    our gnostic bodies not only our own, tidy of step. "One's
    gnostic body not only one's own," we said out loud, the
                                                    Gib-
    let Rim Split truly
    there

One's gnostic body not only one's own was our new
slogan. In the deep dream it turned out we were
in we wrote it on placards. We marched proclaiming it

                                                   true,

     verging, as Itamar took it, on sex-polis. "Only the
beauty of women ever made anything worth a damn,"
    he said, pulled back and put sex aside, pushed back,
pulled away though he had. "Each at our lonely window

                                              oth-

    erwise," he went on, "each on our private perch." "But
not only that," Mrs. P chimed in, "not only that," and we
   all, in turn, piped up, "Not only that," our sway heads

                                              bob-

bling

•

I walked in back of Andreannette as we walked on
the isthmus, her shapely behind my guiding light. A
theme of amplitude lit my brow, I was in church, but-
tock assumption the gospel it all preached. A hollow
                                                    lay
in my stomach, a pitted mood gnostic embodiment
contracted, gnostic suspicion no defense. Andrean-
nette's ass notwithstanding, I felt gnawed at, not not-
withstanding but in line with it perhaps, lure one could
                                                    only
be put upon by… Or was it Nub's fault I wondered,
silly sounding as it was, a momentary lapse lasting ages I
fought Nub with, Nubness in the pits of our stomachs
                                                    we
sought out of, the comb-over's captive audience we'd
been. We no longer were but we were still on planet Nub,
sex-polis death-polis instead. "All Along the Isthmus"
was a song we might've made of it, an ythmic way we'd let
                                                    both

sway our
heads

•

Know-nothing polity drove our blood pressure up.
　Nub's new reality-show host had been stirring
the pot. "Polis broke my heart," Mrs. P complained
　　　　　　　　　　　　　　　　　　　　　and
　　we all amen'd. My gnostic body broke my heart
I wanted to say but I bit my tongue, gnostic body body
　politic went without saying. A pair of hospital socks
　　　　　　　　　　　　　　　　　　　　crept
　　up on me as we walked it felt like, suspect body
cut into again. Suspect body cut into birthing dreams
　of Andreannette, ample as all dream, all having hold…
Not since the Dread Lakes had body been so inured of
　　　　　　　　　　　　　　　　　　　bone.
We trod close to the line, prosodic or genealogical, "the
　line" a loose way of talking we went on talking. "I never
got over learning people die," Anuncio said. "And kill,"
　　　　　　　　　　　　　　　　　　　Sister
　　C put in… We marked our way, song, where there was
one, one of say, never knowing first-hand what it sang,
　the song of what was said to've been, the song of what
　　　　　　　　　　　　　　　　　　　was

　said to've been
said

We continued along the isthmus, the Giblet Rim
Split no joke, history a looting party's alibi as far
  as we could see. Ours were sway heads touched by
                                         tilt,

    bird reckoning. We looked out at what we saw
all the more quizzical, more unbelieving it could ac-
  tually be. A muted trumpet's vibrating razor buzzed
us, our sway heads listed left and right... Aboard a
                                     ship
    afloat at the foot of a mountain, we were we of the
rolling sea, we of the strolling church, high sound our
                                   sign,

    high si-
lence

Huff had us give alchemy another try. Gross
   would go to subtle he said. Dreams of the
Inuit girl whose fingers turned into seals had
                                        kept
      him up all night. It felt good to be awake,
   he said, not just dream-awake… He said he'd
   have combed her disheveled hair with his
fingers, he said her chapped lip cut his lip. He
                                        took
   her to have come from close to the sun, he said,
      decked in Eskimo disguise but a Siddha consort
to the learned eye. Exactly his we were to know
                                        and
      we did. He had heard a flute in the background,
he said, a flute that stayed in the low register, the
   aural counterpart of a ghost. A piece of each note
                                        tore
      loose, he said, mercury moved inside… Huff's
   head floated as he spoke, cut loose from bodily an-
      chorage, guru, elephant goad. One wanted it all
to be like sovereign sex, its give and its get, he said.
                                        He
   spoke of leech-bound mercury, semen and men-
      strual blood, the fragmentary epic of lingam and
yoni. Kundalini lay on his tongue enjoying meat, alco-
   hol and fish, to eat and to speak a lubricity of sorts,
                                        he
said. We had a sense we'd been moving in circles. It
   made us dizzy we felt it so, epic fragment broken off
   and set adrift with no way home, only a faint sense
                                        home
   ever
   was

•

The long march Giblet Rim Split had been stayed
with us. We put our legs into listening to Huff, our
  backs hurt, our mortal bodies our closer walk. Huff
                                                    was
    every breath we took. He spoke to our every un-
  derlying wish, that the body abide forever foremost.
    He addressed us as a hoopoe to all other birds.
                                              "Dear
  Birds," we heard him say... But we were not birds
    or not often enough, the diminution of Nub that the
spite prez won our diminution, so hard not to see it
                                                  that
    way. Huff's head was in fourteenth-century India,
      far from sex polis-death polis, gun-lobby polis Nub.
Con alma, we said even so. Con alma, we said all the
  more so, mercury the rutting elephant hoisted high on
                                              Huff's
    tongue. It wasn't we were thinking soul was on our
  side, thinking that soul took sides. Con alma, we kept say-
    ing, emptied of all but ythmic import, bird food it might
have been. "Dear Birds," we heard Huff say again, a book of
                                                    tan-
    tric flight on his tongue... The root of bliss piled up on his
      tongue, as did nectar and the three sweets, mercury's auspi-
cious ornament, six-limbed yoga, Lotus-Navel. It seemed a
                                                    nom-
inative science he espoused, all of us reaching for what the
    names meant, Nub's flight from meaning no matter, Nub's
                                                        flight
  all the reason
more

To confer was to be birds and to fly to conspire deeply.
  To go from gross to subtle was to fly counter to
Nub's flight, Nur's flight, but not just that, the Giblet

                                            Rim
    Split barely a memory by now. Spirit's worldly reach
  told of empty splendor, the inconsequence of earthly
  fire no matter it urged it, did so thru Huff holding forth.

                                            "Just
    know," it seemed it said and he said, double talk braid-
    ed in say long since, a forked way north of say... We made
    book as on a bet, a book of antiphonal sway, no known

                                            con-
  sequence no
matter

ITAMAR'S GIBLET REDUX

—"mu" two hundred eighteenth part—

He lay in the dark foreday morning remember-
ing his body's better days. He had died and briefly
looked back on the world, all of it continuing,

        as

he was not. It was ribcage theater but worse,
a certain something gotten into his lungs. The
room smelled of sublimated blood and semen,

        the

room and the atmosphere he called his lab. A
surly alchemy he proposed it all came down to,
a snarl caught on the side of his mouth... A dole-
ful music sightread from no book arose from the

        book

Andreannette sat reading, sweet Andreannette
in whose lap the book lay, the book that was of her
lap, was her lap, all of it his could he have music's

        way

with the world. Such was its way with love's chem-
iatric emissions, Itamar's Hindu roots by way of Brazil,
waft a mere "eye" short of music, remnant nuzzle,

        rem-

nant musk, each the epic fragment soul caught...
Soul sought, never again not looking, eye shy not-
withstanding. Soul reeled and recoiled, come thru
Giblet Rim Split, no one wanting to know what it

        was,

what soul was, played on by sarod, tablas, tam-
boura, the airs of Itamar's youth. Manifold elations
of breath and breathlessness, a madrigal of seem-
ing retreat the way Andreannette sat madonnalike...

        A

certain weight it all got, him having headed grave-
ward, gravitas we called it, staring out. Lengths of
string sat caught in our stomachs as we the chorus,

        the

would-be chorus, looked on. We were so wanting
to call it Gizzard Rim Split, having come not know-
ing why and gone away still not knowing. We all sat

        whil-

ing, "While we're here" on the tips of our tongues,
Andreannette's goddesslike apportionment phonemic
   now, a sound Itamar heard as much as a sight he saw,

                                                      an

aroma each phoneme fell loaded with, pheromonal bait
   it seemed… Gone from gross to subtle reluctantly
he confessed, grown sublime at his prostate's expense.

                                                      An-

   dreannette he called his lab assistant, shot thru like
perfume in a flower and he as well, their bodies thru
   the heat of their austerities oblatory, their bodies were
they as they would have them be. Bound mercury broke

                                                      and

   fell into epic fragments, each the legendary meeting of
essence and accident, chorded sulfur's throw of the
dice what went for love. He was alchemy's mouthpiece.

                                                      Much

   to be thought about rolled off his tongue: a moon well
belching fire, the one drop of white-red nectar, the five
   ways of going away, other pentads appertaining. Steve

                                                      Cole-

   man came on the box… We made of the wish-fulfill-
ing cow and the sky-going circle what we could, red mini-
um, lineage nectar and the two mouths what we could.

                                                      We

made of the essences mixed in the cranial vault what we
   could, the recumbent sojourner what we could. We made
of all of them what we could or we just went along, grades

                                                      and

   degrees yet to be come to
we knew

———————————

Mercury said to've dripped from a pigeon's beak
he spoke of next. It lay on the ground, lapped up by a
snake representing lead. It was an inauspicious day.
                                                                    It
     was Friday the 13th. He put what Monk had made
of it on the box, cheered up. Smeared fluids on his
     feet gave him wings he dreamt, base to gold again…
                                                                    To
        airlift out of Nub and its trouble with color, to let
     it suffer its apprentice prez a bitter alchemy, vitriol
        no matter the matter, funny looked at from a star. We
the would-be chorus understood, made of it what we
                                                            could,
     we the under voice could we have spoken or sung, the
        polis voice, the polis antiphony, polis low groan or
     degree… The base of the medial channel wanted to be
                                                            open
     we were told, acolytes in a New School of Tantric Re-
     dress, the new name truth's abidance went by. We saw
        mercury of the ether, ethereal, sulfur bring a direness to
                                                            life,
        a directness, antiphonal adept it seemed. Fish belly got
     spoken of, diaphragmatic retention, this the very least as
                                                            oth-
        er austerities rolled off his
     tongue

•

Able to look thru the world as well as at it, the
    visionary prospect he proclaimed, mumbling
into his hand off to one side. He saw all the way to
                                                            An-
    dhra Pradesh and on into nowhere, he said, blood
    and cloth boiled in a vat of milk, a pot broken
in the world. What we made of it laid out a highway
                                                        of
symbols, a metaphorical highway the literal intruded
    on. A deadly pileup we rode past gave us pause.
    "Peace be upon us," we begged as though we were
                                                    dead...
    Breath retained as in a pot he went on about next,
teachings brought down at Moon Mountain. The moon
    grew glad at such tutelage's behest, its and Itamar's
                                                        list-
    ing to the left. Our heads grew light at the men-
    tion of Moon Hill, Moon Mountain, a mountain with
    its feet in the water, the moon the left nostril took
us to, my head not the least light among them. I floated
                                                        high
    above bodily complaint, legs intact again, no matter
    a taste of hopeless love came back to me, a dream or
    a thought of Andreannette Absconditus Itamar sparked,
her by another name I thought I'd forgotten, no sooner
                                                        re-
    collected than it slipped away... Wilted rose. True epic
    fragment. An unstrung lute's relay. It all pressed on
me as Itamar spoke, Andreannette's namesake mesh his
                                                        and
    my nemesis, the mixed-emotional warrant mercuric
sulfide was known to issue, me a would-be chorus of
    one. "The little bell," I kept repeating, "the little bell,"
                                                        a
wrinkle yanked out of the air. His were teachings over-
    heard inside a fish's belly I heard Itamar say, wine
    thrown into the water. So much detail it all took I fell
                                                        back
    reeling, my would-be chorus of one our would-be cho-
rus again, absorbed into the we again... He was on the part

about Andreannette's legs when I came back in, legs, he
                                                  said,
   like the trunks of plan-
tain trees

"Everything is everything," I heard myself say,
harkening back to a gentler time. So it seemed at
   least, not being there now, now no longer the one
                                          we
      once were in. Another part of me or an entire
   me sank as that part of me or an entire me floated,
      the thought or the wish being we go back to being
   God when we die. All aspiration welled up in my
                                          throat,
         all obstruction, all strain. To sing was to cough,
      clear one's throat or try to, expectorate forever,
         all the fire of time, song as though dragged out of
                                          me,
   would-be no longer would-be… I heard Itamar even
      so. The base where the well of heaven had its opening
      spoke thru him, thin as a thread, the cranial heavens
                                          his
         bent albeit carnal, rejuvenant woods between Andre-
      annette's legs. The woods turned into nectar held in
         his head, his head a tej bar, the restored Ethiopian of
                                          lore
      none other than
   him

As if to declaim atop dunduns and synth, Itamar
   waxed beautifully announcing mercury had
been given a mouth, sweat come out where hair

                                               root-
   ed, the sublimity such that Tête, bone-chested
Tête, yelled, "But what about Nub?" It was a coun-
   terweight she wanted to be, alchemico-yogic
sublimity's foil, the pull of polis... Waves broke

                                            among
   the pilings under the pier we found ourselves on.
   Stagger was only a step, he said, a dance of imbal-
ance of a sort. He said gold was an Elysian polis's

                                              arri-
   vancy he saw, lead the apprentice prez's base.
Concord he called it, not only honey in the head he
   said, at which Tête took offense but he went on...

                                               We
would be cooked by our austerities, he said, by way of

                                            trans-
   verse distillation over-
come

So much about the base in the air, the base against
  the subtle what polis was, polis's lost cause our
lament. The box had moved on from Monk's Friday.

                                      Brass
  adamance cut with ricochet was back. Earl Cross
walked into the tej bar looking like a trumpet, a Master
at last. He walked like Itamar emerging from woods

                                     that
  were women's thighs… There was tej or indeed
nectar raining down. Sublimated mercury's ambrosial
  clime came in with him, a new tune's head he was

                                  always

hearing

ANUNCIO'S FOURTEENTH LAST LOVE SONG

—"mu" two hundred nineteenth part—

Anuncio sat up high in the cranial heavens,
   humped high, as he'd once read, vaulted
up. Something seen in a face, Anuncia's face,
                                    ratch-
      eted the air. Pure thought or mere thought,
         he told himself, an alchemical conceit drawn
from the book of the wet of kisses, renuncia-
tive conceit, vulvic emission what was meant
                                          by
      kiss, had gone to his head. Goaded by Huff
and Itamar as if he were mercury. Root lock.
   Feathered lock. Net-bearing lock... Tantric re-
straint. Abdominal retention. Fire lay with fire,
                                       cal-
   cinatory finesse. Not so much a last love song
as a last Nub song he sang, mundane volleys repet-
   itive, "Done got tired," he announced, wanting
                                          out.
      He spoke as if a kiss were stuck in his mouth,
   Anuncia's teeth and tongue caught in his throat,
      goaded by talk of womanly sulfur, rice grains, bar-
leycorns, lye, wash water, a tricklesome theology of
                                             ashes,
      rice balls eaten by the dead... It was an almost ul-
         timate song. Anuncia looked on, listened in, the
scars on Anuncio's body not forgotten lying under his
   clothes. He sat entranced by an odor on the tips of
                                             his
fingers. She sat entranced by a sound no one could
   hear, an emanation from the nonmanifest one
   heard Itamar call it. A shaded substrate of sound
                                          one
      heard him call it. A phonematic lowest of the
low one heard him call it, lifted, one heard him say,
   by the vertebrae snake. It was all only what it
seemed, what could be made with say, the almost
                                          ulti-
      mate song Anuncio sang, all as if only something

left in our throats… Residue. Afterthought. Philo-
sophic phlegm. The alchemical stone worn down to
                                                    an
    alum, dust where tonsils
    had been

                    •

    There stood a stadial amending of things to their
mention, so much had the myth or the science of
    it progressed, a new page in *The Book of So* none
                                                    of
    us expected. Anuncio sat counting sheep, each
with its true correlative: rod, leech, crow droppings,
    whey, butter, sphere, a bridge made of hair… He
                                                    was
    heard to say to himself, "Swallow my mouthful,"
    a prompt, an apparent proffer. A Kemetic-alchemi-
cal contagion came over him, Itamar the Ethiopian
                                                Egyp-
    tian, the Pharaoh's black torso blacker than the
        blackest black, the cattle fields of Dendera open-
ing his nose… A transitional chord, a passing tone,
    a stepping-stone lapis, a last love song number seven
                                                    times
    two. Something of the Paleolithic Venuses about
Anuncia moved him, bolted by yogic stasis though he
    was. Something seen in her face that wasn't there,
something seen in her hips, knees, calves, ankles. Was
                                                    it
    a real or a would-be song we began to wonder, asking
        whose witnesses were we, what word whose amen
    we were… A last love song number forty-two times two
                                                    di-
    vided by six. A faint Sanskrit inscription he imagined he
    saw on a slice of bread, six lentil's-weight of breath in
                                                    the
    scale pan, the world coming
    apart

•

A last love song number six times seven di-
   vided by three, was it the last Osirian remnant
was the question, Itamar what but a whisper in
                                A-

nuncio's ear. They would meet that night at
noon was the plan, his and her reverse coition
   clear the mind, ears dropped into by pebbles of
                                light,

   mercury possessed of a mouth… We leaned
in, listening, the sounded hollows known as clari-
   nets all up into us. Anuncia no virgin on horse-
back we knew, was it all only, we wondered, legend,
                               lore.

   Everything receded, said to've been said to've
     been said to've been said, all of it into the mystic,
into the quotidian again. It was all about angles, all
                            about

   nothing, a summative something not to be offered
up… Come to a late stage of love, snake nectar, Itamar
   promised, a remote mountain said to've been taken
into his head or him to've been taken up into a mountain.
                                He

   was our would-be chorus's whisperer. An atmospheric
   station awaited us he promised. Nub was not our
limit, he vowed, high arts of corruption come to roost
                              no

   matter, a soap nut filled with mercury, borax, etc.,
sealed with molasses and lime, would prevail… Such
   the good news he proffered, such the news we were
                              to

relay

We stood transfixed, no end to our astonishment.
  The cosmos came toward us outfitted with a torso,
a head, limbs. Clarinets blew behind us, we the
                                        would-
    be many, would-be most. That the broken earth
would prove or pay down on integral heaven, a shat-
  terproof pot its image or symbol but plastic, we
                                        com-
    plained... Itamar had come out of caves boast-
  ing cranial ceilings. Thick Venuses he'd seen play-
    ing volleyball came back to him, midriffs, hips and
thighs distilling elixir. Vulval essence Huff called it,
                                        Sophia
    called it the real thing, long silent but at last inter-
      vening, genital emission a theophany of late... Put-
ting his mouth to Anuncia's mouth, calling her nether
  mouth her mouth, Anuncio called himself a latter-day
                                        Tan-
    trist, called it the smear of
love

We the chorusing few were laryngitic by now,
   clarinets blithe in the background piping anew,
bracing for our voices' return. Anuncio braced
                                   as
   well, rock water put into an oil bath under his
tongue, lack of attributes a virtue it appeared…
   Itamar counseled him, reincarnated out of India,
                             yogic
     seed carried up to the top of an alcove under his
     brow. Pure phlegm climbed up his throat… We were
     each only our lone apocalypse, partial truth that
   bore buttressing, so weak we all were, fractal epiphany
                                 more

   than anyone
knew

"Dearly Beloved" was on the box as we pulled
   in, *took between my lips* translated *took between*
my legs, cusp of tongue translated *bodily thrust,*
                           A-
   nuncia's recension of late. No Council of Ni-
caea approved it but could we have been that
   Council, testamental affray not our intent. Anun-
cia's peasant blouse highlighted her bosom, sweet
                           ro-
   tundities one lapped at, looking. She sat at the
wheel as we descended from the bus, young again,
   the eldress to come etched into her face… There
                         was
no telling where it was we disembarked, Anuncia's
   late recension a new frontage only she knew, sacro-
sanct love all the more sacrosanct,   a beloved
                        sphinc-
   ter gripping a beloved finger celestial mechan-
ics,   all the more the more down it got. It was all
so much wood she went thru like a saw, valedic-
tory advance could it be called an advance. An appen-
dix in *The Book of So* it might've been, so's way
                    of
owning incumbency, *took between* having always
   been… Bodily delight. Bodily dismay. Resplendent
wood's metaphysical dementia… Who was to say it
                   was-
   n't hell's own pleasure, a faint waft of sulfur demand-
ed to know,   who not to name it Nub's buttock fix,
   the world's buttock fix. So said none other than the son
                   of
the philosophers it appeared, so said or said as much
                  the
   philosopher's
stone

Anuncio the Sulfurous Ethiopian he proclaimed him-
    self, last love song singer par excellence, Anuncio
E, Anuncio X. Primitive exchange not to be solved
                                                but
    exacerbated, odoriferous advent toward an alter-
nate world. Mr. Poot-Butt she called him, reeling
    him back to earth,   she of the inquiring finger,
he of the inviting behind, an alchemical tryst with
                                                sul-
    fur, him the natural sulfur,   an elixir of youth
    to be found... So went the recension they grew to
love and we to listen to, reading the book out loud,
                                                a
    tantric swath cut across the expanse we stepped
off the bus into, DISPLAY OF LEG AND SLAPPING OF
    THIGHS GINNING GENITAL TREE SAP the name the
                                                sign
    said it went
by

The passing of gas a divine afflatus, the male
sulfur, a species of ether, a quick spout of spi-
ritual instruction. Was that what it meant, did

                                      they
    dare go there, we asked each other, we the
    would-be chorus,   were we to know his and
    her pungent fingertips as none other than the

                                       pre-
mises of love. The never not susceptible body,
    was that what she was getting at, they were
getting at, we asked as one, truly a chorus now,

                                 car-
    oling for keeps…   We heard Gato's broken
heart on the box in back of us, a grave music, so

                              much
    to mourn, so much to la-
ment

_____

(7.xi.17: out of nowhere)

Again I dreamt I lay at the foot of Mount Ida,
  a moment's declaration of love taken back.
"I think about you often," I confessed. She was
                                   the
  muse of my youth as before, late teens, early
twenties, her namesake mountain clear code, my-
  self no Zeus, me atop the mountain my thrill...
                                   We
  lay naked on a nondescript bed, haunting my
  old age,   she of the tight chest, me of the heavy
  hand, the dream no more than what might have
                                 been

was-
n't

We were wanting to sing love, not Nub, our
   night on the mountain braced us. We slept
  close to the sky, we saw stars thru closed
                                  eye-
  lids. Braced by the cold, we awoke and
took down our tents, in the singing so soon
  it scared us, into the singing, the toned or
                                  at-
  tuned bevel the air hummed with, none
of us not with perked ears, taking note…
  Twelve score plus one the song it was, the
                                 sing-
ing we were in, the number we said let's call
  it, nothing but number to go on, song twelve
  score plus one, otherwise only the singing.
                                Our
heads hummed without name other than num-
  ber heading down the mountain, tents packed
  up and put away, back on the bus… News of
                                an-
  other shooting spree came on the radio, the
song we were singing, wanting to sing, pushed
  back in our throats. Nominative and numer-
ical ran as one coming down the mountain, the
                               num-
  ber of dead naming something, the number of
  wounded likewise, no other way to say either,
such the way Nub was, number alone the name
                                of
  it, number alone spoke, something not to be
named, naming nothing… Twenty-six dead, twen-
ty wounded. Three to the third minus one, two
                              times
  ten. Fifty-two divided by two, four times five.
Nine squared minus three divided by three, four
  squared plus four. Four into one hundred four,
eight squared minus eleven times four. What to say,
                             what
  to say, what number won't say. Somewhere in
  Texas, the radio said. Nub, number, numb… The

singing offset it some, followed us down the moun-
tain, the beveled air gotten into our heads beyond

                                                         re-
moval, our heads into our ears, inside and out. The
singing buzzed us, the song's number name our de-
fault on naming, not wanting to presume. It was

                                     the
hum of the mountain woods, the high hum of
having been to the mountain. Beveled address hard-
ly began to say what it was to be in it, a something

                                          that
might not have been something, abstract entangle-
ment, a getting of getting gone thin. I wanted a
horse-trot batá sound for its translation, the singing

                                          an
orisha far north. I wanted my dream of Mount Ida
to have portended it, would-be mount I lay at whose
feet looking up into thicket, tantric swath cut across it

                                                all
still

          •

Sister C called herself Queen of the Mountain, a
typical effect, everyone knew, of coming down.
We were on a descent whose consequences were

                                          leg-
end. We all said, "Be that." We all said, "Go
ahead. Be that." Hers was the hand that burst out
of a pillar, she said, like a shoot sprouting out

                                         of
a tree. Hers was the hair, she said, one reached
for while asleep… We were clearly crossing the
tantric swath. She spoke of mustard seeds, lamps

                                         lit
by mustard oil, rancid butter. She said she was
goat-headed with bell-shaped ears. The hyperanima-
cy of the spirits was in play. Djed spoke next, a pure
peyote-button baritone, much having been heard of

                                         "that
which is arisen from the basin," of "that which is
to be raised into the head," of "the End of the Five
Times Twelve," these as well well-known effects of

                                         com-

ing down… We rolled down the mountain, part ava-
   lanche, part runaway horse. He pounded his chest and
proclaimed, "I am the Emitter, the divine and demonic

                             Sid-

   dha of yore," the resplendence of tantric swath get-
ting to him. He reminisced about an undertaker's daugh-
ter, her pubic triangle, he said, a secret without equal,

                           not

   to be divulged, then harkened back to another he
called the ungrateful one, garlanded by the sky, he
   said, even in full array, "garlanded by the sky" a way
of saying "naked." Redwood and manzanita went by

                        as

we continued our descent, "played by Putin" a scrap
   of news heard on the radio in the background, oak
went by as well. Something got said between Djed and

                      Sis-

   ter C about the crooked one, the bent-over one who
licked her own biscuit. Seed and secretion came up
   as well… We wondered was our descent the drop of

                    love,

   the tantric drop that Huff preached and Sophia pro-
selytized, that Itamar and Andreannette proclaimed.
   We turned off the news. "Ganesh Sound" had been on

                  the

box and we went back to it, David S. Ware's renuncia-
   tive moan. Sequoia went by as we went down the moun-
tain, hemlock and mahogony as well. Birch went by, ash

                 and

   pinyon as well, jupiter and fir, cottonwood, dogwood
and alder. Talk of gnostic flow, gnostic fluidity, passed
   between Djed and Sister C, word of some who drank the

                  wa-

   ter in which her biscuit had been bathed… The outer
entourage of a sudden, were we the drop of love, Nub
   notwithstanding, we wondered, to leave a mark among
the misbegotten, we ourselves misbegotten, our descent

                  the

   very drop of love. Maple went by, laurel and buckeye
as well… We saw ourselves in our tantric incompleteness,
   childless mothers' motherless children for the space of

                  com-

ing down

In this sense, the Tantric practitioner is a crypto-potentate, transacting like a king with the boundless energy of the godhead that flows from the elevated center of his worship mandala. Here, then, we see that the utopia of the Tantric mandala may serve both to ground legitimate royal authority and power when the king is a Tantric practitioner, as well as to subvert illegitimate power or create a covert nexus of power when the wrong king or no king is on the throne.

—David Gordon White, *Kiss of the Yogini:*
   "Tantric Sex" in its South Asian Contexts

STAINLESS LOTUS OF LIGHT

—*"mu" two hundred twenty-first part*—

Mr. P stood quarreling with the Mrs. He let a tear
   drop to the floor, gnostic fluidity, gnostic flow.
He stood thinking about tantric romance. He stood
                                             hav-
      ing just come down from the mountain, he stood
   busted up as though he'd never gone up the moun-
      tain. Thoughts and prayers lay busted, broken, bits
                                             of
   glass under his feet wherever he stepped... Nub's
      faux republic warred without remedy, God was gun.
   Were they Nub's live ammo, he wondered, watching
                                             it as
      well as in it. Thoughts and prayers lay spoken of
   out of every mouth, behind every podium. Everyone
had been up and still everyone scattered, he and she
   no less, he lamented, the drop of love a drop of blood
                                             fall-
      en from his eye... Thoughts and prayers lay kicked
   about, no goddess's kiss, no worshipful address, we
      the would-be chorus asking what but stealth polis was,
                                             Nub's
      new realty-show prez getting to us, what but grab, klep-
   tocratic whim. Next to nothing what there was to fight
      about no matter, he and the Mrs., inured in their Nubness,
   fought. He heard a flamenco singer singing about Plato
                                             he

thought, thoughts easy to come by, prayers easy to
   come by… We the would-be chorus fell back mum,
having none of it, tantric romance come down to grabbed-
at lotuses, bad rhyme inside out. So said the book of
                                             mem-
   ory we were in or would be in, no not looking back.
They were quarreling over who was the king though
   there was no king, people with eyes too big for their
                                             fac-
   es, an imp of aggrievement egging them on. We the
witnessing raff, wanting to sing but silent, leaned in,
   love's royal conjugant would-be royal, root of all puta-
tiveness, let-go, longed-after mesh… This the war Mr.
                                             and
   Mrs. found themselves in. Tantric polity. Tantra's wet
   eucharist. A prince composed of pieces what princi-
pality. "To write a Republic in gloom," we'd read. This
                                             was
   that

                        •

   A royal couple could they have reconciled, reached
agreement, the testing and the teasing of the Who'd-
Have-Thought Church, the one she'd be queen in, the
                                             one
   he'd be whose king, the twisting and the shouting
and the working of it out. "Blue Star" was on the
   box as we leaned in, the chorus, it turned out, we'd
                                             have
   been. Hawkins's horn plied a kind of hoarse weep-
      ing. Carter was reasoning, wanting to reason, trying
to reason with the way of things, blue suppliant, blue
                                             de-
   tente… No mountain figment was it, Mr. P kept say-
ing, their dreamt, gone-after royalty real, Mrs. P ask-
   ing what he'd been smoking. Benny Carter's appeal to
                                             rea-
   son played on us all, his cosmic petition. We too had
been to the mountain, we remembered, were of the moun-
   tain as we were there, but the box took one's voice
away, put membranes, hammers, horns and strings in its
                                             place.

We the would-be chorus remained would-be, Mr. and
  and Mrs. P went on as ever. "Tell me to place your
feet on my shoulders," he told her, "and look you up and
                                                    down."
    "Blue Star" gave way to "Blue Nile," soup-cooler flutes
  at our backs had our backs, a long having-to-do-with-it no
                                                    sum-
    ming-up could
  serve

So went the ins and outs of the Who'd-Have-Thought
   Church. He was asking which of his earlier lives
had she been his wife in, this as they sat crosslegged
                                          fac-
   ing each other, waft from their love parts widening
their nostrils, excited against their wills... She told him
   it wasn't Nepal they were in, not the Middle Ages
                                          they
      were in. We the would-be chorus leaned in, drawn
   by a tableau so bleak our reckoning eyes bled, a tes-
      tament equally bleak drawn out of us, loudly no lon-
ger would-be... "The wrong king," we intoned again
                                          and
   again. We read from a book, more hymnal than book
      the way we read it, operatic, more like a libretto,
nothing not affected by Nub's lost facelift... Grabbed
                                          hair,
      grabbed lips, grabbed opening, desecrated yoni...
   Nub's new apprentice prez stumbling in the doorway,
                                          court

      clown were he not
king

•

Quixotic talk of Water-Pot Mountain and Black Bee
   Cave we leaned in on, of yellow footprints left on a
rock. There was talk of emission and retraction,
                                             air-
   borne mothers and lords of the fields, our lapsar-
ian demidivinity there to be gotten back, might ritual
   make it more than bodily regard. We the would-be
                                             cho-
   rus, he the would-be king, she the would-be god-
dess, consort, queen… They would be royalty in a
   compensatory court she wanted nothing to do with,
calling themselves tantra though they were not. So it
                                             was
   we put our two cents in, we the parachronicle choir,
      thought thinking outside itself providing what spoke
inside. There grew talk of an eighth continent quadri-
sected by the four Mountains of Black Antinomy, one
                                             of
which we wanted Abdullah's Mountain of the Night to
   be. The far shore of the Rock Water River, whose touch
turns one to stone, got mention as well, so deep were we
                                             into
   the whatsaid realm, the moon an upside-down umbrella
      Mr. P put on our foreheads… Quizzical itch, conniption,
   quiver, spillage. Our thoughts migrated to the birdlegged
                                             boy,
muni-bird amenities off in the distance, kleptocratic polis,
   token vote. Mr. P wanted to overcome, as we all did,
   wanted to be that bird, the compensative, would-be king,
                                             he-
   ro king. We the parachoric brigade were with him now,
Miles Davis in Europe on the box, "Autumn Leaves," we
   swung so hard we swang. We fingerpopped so hard we dis-
located our thumbs, thugs loose, Kali Yuga no matter, many
                                             an
   austerity sublimed. By way of the four bodily arrays, we
   explained to Mrs. P, Mr. P had impregnated himself, big now
   with kingship, that he and she rise to their higher evolutes,
                                             wings
   made of calcinated mer-
cury

Mr. P had gone off, Mrs. P complained. He was wanting
    to be up to alchemy, wanting to be king. He was wanting
it to be as he'd read, quixotic, wanting it to be as it never

                                                was.
    He had called her his wagtail woman, up from which he
        promoted her to queen… He was trying to fictionalize
himself, we semisang explaining, he was trying to be of the

                                                book,
        adding what only a tantric jazz chorale could add or in-
    timate, each the pervading agent who never blinks we'd be if

                                                we
could

No wonder he went off, we semisang, the wonder
was not everyone did. Nub gone over to the hands
of the guilty, we were sulfurous, fuming, wondering
                                                    what
    to do, the other side cheated, won. We were licking
our wounds, biting at scabs, the alchemico-acidic nextet,
                                                        spite
    choir, vitriol's mantric
dress

I dozed off led by stringent perfume, synaes-
thetic light, pent arousal all inner ignition. It was
   a dream of Andreannette sought me out, her

                                    plush,
      night-nursical givingness, girth, come to
   after fret, much runaround. She was the one she
   might've been more than the one she was, a
sense of contentment between us, fraught though

                                         it'd
      been before. I saw her "shining like new money"
   but matte at the same time, news of another life…
It was Insofar-I's dream, I knew, not mine. He was

                                    dream-
      ing about the she she no longer was and had nev-
      er been. I scratched my head until a word fell out,
eked-out consonance's boon but enough. He was
   dreaming of a home he'd never been to, Andrean-
   nette native there, the savagery of Nub up in his

                                         face
      no matter, a dreamt coming-to come true… In-
   sofar-I. Insofar-She. Neither could have said they were
   asleep. All he knew was home had her look, she had

                                       home's
   look, grandmother, mother, sister, wife. Grandmother,
   mother, sister, wife, an early grade school teacher.
Churchical something like cervical again, something like

                                           u-
      terine again. Even so, we were drinking melted-icecap
      daquiris, the multiform we she, he and I also were, the
rage of the earth in our cartilage and fingertips, connois-
   seurs of disaster, defeat. An alter-Andreannette loomed like

                                            the
      earth itself, I surmised, auguring abiding dread. Never
not missing home, which wasn't there, deportees we might

                                           've

      been

•

We the would-be choir chimed in, becoming devo-
tional, never not there, never not elsewhere, bent on
being in but not of. Why we stuttered, why we were

                                                stut-
   tering, what but words to go there with. Something
seen in a face no face had ever made good on had
   us going. We spoke perched on our bodies' decline,

                                                semi-
   sang, singing for the people who felt the same way,
John Lee might well have been on the box... Death
   tracked us we knew but put a strong face on, some-
thing anyone saw was all front. This it was gave word of

                                                our
common condition, this our closer walk was with. We
   bowed our heads awaiting the blade on our necks, amid
all of which Andreannette came to me in a dream, a night

                                                nurse
   I'd've had to be Gregory Isaacs to do justice to, all
grist and unexpectedness come out right... There'd been
   a patient who died who said he'd soon be out of their

                                                way
   was back among them she said. I felt a trembling as
of the world and the way of the world, I detected move-
   ment such as would've been meant by spirit, what mean-
ing was to be made of it held in abeyance, the meaning its

                                                be-
   ing held in abey-
ance

_____

Stick City incense burned in my room, a waft of
which conjured hips, tight crevices, hair, all that
   lay between. Andreannette stood at my bedside, a
                                             deep
      singing sounding like shadows of a voice, gruff
   murmur, immanence caught between limbs of a
   tree outside. She made it not being alright seem
                                             al-
right, spirit's endowment, a cut she said something
   over, made better, kissed... There was a creak-
   ing of the spirit I thought I heard, rickety wind or a
                                             rick-
      etiness foisted by the wind, what was not to be had
I heard. There was a rattliness fostered by the wind,
   the room a shaken cage, a rickety hip howling making
                                             me

   howl

My night nurse Andreannette came to my bedside,
  big of breast and of bodily affection, real no matter
I dreamt it, more real. My rickety hip migrated to

                                             In-
    sofar-I's pelvis, blessed by Andreannette's gar-
  landed phonemes, vulval underneath it all. Not since
night-nursical fell off my tongue had I felt it so.

                                      All
  I wanted was to linger in the crease apprehending
    it made, never having extracted from so far down...
Even so, the howl escaped me, a yelp like the one I

                                            let
  out bitten by my dog. Song three times nine squared
    we were calling it, song three to the fifth we called it
as well, an algorithmic mend underneath it all beyond

                                           our
    ken. We breathed in our most intimate aromas, al-
  gorithmic mention, Whitmanian sweat. Matthew Shipp
    came on the box, a sprinkling of pixie dust, spectral
countrysides we crossed, become skeletal, skeletal drift

                                           we
    strayed at large in, the call of what loomed ahead,
  what ailed us what limned our way... Not until Andre-
annette yelled at William Parker's bowed bass was

                                          our
  traipse broken. "Scratch it like an itch!" Andreannette
    yelled. "Itchy skin wants ritual!" she yelled when
she yelled again. Itchy skin's metaphorical itch wanted

                                           rit-
    ual, it wanted friction, scratch, rub. Ritual wanted pos-
    ture, an abutment out at arm's length, want up over
  itself unbeknownst. This was the way with our Stick City

                                            rit-
    ual, real but all inside. Stick City intaglio. Stick City itch,
itch's increase. Stick's metaphoric surmise. Ritual's advance

                                          over
    instinct, buffeted before us a-
  gain

Revisitation was ritual's way, algebraic mend
   and mention. A manic circling beset us, we the
obsessed, our trek so disconsolate we wept. A
                                        choked-
   up arpeggio visited our throats. Was it some-
how fear could make the thing we fear happen we
   walked wondering, Nub so mean of late… Out
                                        of
   bed, I walked hit on the head and it hummed.
Hum was a sort of honey, sweet consonance I'd've
   said, the slap it issued from no matter. The slap
                                        was
   a sip at Andreannette's lip I made-believe, compen-
      sative sip an insistent comp as upon a piano, pianistic
touch an infatuation with cloth, what cloth covered,
                                        ritu-

   al's remnant
glow

Huff gave me a frame for it. Andreannette sat
  beside Insofar-I's bed. Insofar-I took her hand
into his. He lay in the cancer clinic alchemy lab,
                                              the
  I that would not be. Recumbent Osiris he might-
've been, baby Moses, baby Krishna, might've been
  as I might've been... Huff gave me a frame for it.
                                              Ma-
    caw plied phonemic flap, mockingbird flap. Not
since Quag had there been such disarray, not that
    Quag had ever left or that we had left Quag. Crater
was Quag inside out... "Insofar" was something we
                                              said
  and then said again, said again and again. We were
    iterative, ontic, etiological, as if say-it-again-said-it-
                                              again
    said some-
thing

I had taken Andreannette in, insofar'd her, Huff,
when I told him, explained. Alchemico-tantric subli-
mation he had in mind. An Insofarian masque it

                                          might-

' ve been... Insofar as there was a where it was
elsewhere, there but on its way there, in-between...
Insofar-I's parallax track. Insofar-I's pent-up twin.

                                                 An-

dreannette blended with Netsanet now, sulfur's Ethio-
   pic advent transformative... Parroted amendment...
   Parroted amends... Masque, mark, mock... Mask...

                                                 Ma-

caw

ITAMAR, REJUVENANT SPOOK

—"mu" two hundred twenty-third part—

We were still in the realm of the said-to've-
    been-said, out at which removes words were
all fluidity, "love's lunar digit" lingered on
                                         Ita-
    mar's tongue. A certain snake lay sleeping
he'd heard, he the man of its dreams, it the
    woman of his, given so greedy a kiss nothing
                                         re-
    mained... He dreamt a dream of such come-
liness it all acquired finish, finesse, womanly
    array and raiment. A certain calm ensued. A
                                      cer-
tain sadness came over it all. We stood, even
    so, and swore by Itamar's book. All our hopes
were bound up there. The soul's vicissitudes
                                  we'd
    come to address, pondering all bodily com-
    mand it came under, all the would-be ones we
were, all of it brought to light. No matter he called
    it *The Book of Inconsequence*, contra *The Book*
                                   of
    So, we were so's devotees and his at the same
time, both books leaned our way... The books
    were two heads fighting Nub's head, Nub's new
head on backwards, Nublican connivance not to
                                 re-
    treat or to be quieted with a kiss, unhappy dead
    we were governed by. The two heads led us
along an ythmic trek, "mythopoepic" Itamar at
                               one
    point called it, "musicopoepic" after that. He
reminisced a lost love, the way she'd worn her hair,
    lamenting that life was that way, unassuming hair
                                  tied
in a bun, gathered up only to be let down... So spoke
    the one book, disempowered, hating even having
    to fight back... So it spoke, a speck of dust on a ball
                                   of
    dust

·

Spoke as if to be done with corporeal things. Dou-
   bling the book pursued some elusive truth, we
intuited, not at liberty to speak otherwise. As if to
                                                    be

   done with blood, bone, meat, sinew... The cave
   sleep turned out to be... The clarity of the day, first
   lit-upon proffer, the starkness first light brought
                                                    in...

Itamar held forth like a ghost or as if he'd seen
   one, himself decked out in white, migratory soul
more see-thru horse than he'd imagined, never to
                                                    be

   known in advance. He had begun to fade, begun
to go out, he felt, bordering on theft, himself even,
   so depleted it seemed, qualified, insofar. Itamar the
                                                    Re-

   juvenant Spook we named as we called him, he
   the intestate one, not we, calling out to him, calling
   him back, flamenco's bad mouth blackening the
sky, cante jondo's boca maldita's first flight, his Our
                                                    Lady

   of the Lower Lip, distant lore... "The day on which
it all became clear," he kept repeating all the same. Wine
   pocked his mouth as he spoke, the day's clarity a black
                                                    res-

   in he spat
   out

•

Ours was the one drop, of which we were many,
   the knots of the subtle body not so. One atom
when in the heart, two when in the throat, three on
                                                    the
      tip of the tongue. "Close upon death," one had
         heard it put. The day whose clarity blinded... The
day one saw it first... The day on which one saw...
                                                    Short
      on string, we strummed our birdcage thoraces, rib-
cage theater play. "A poverty of resource," we'd al-
so heard, an expectorant phlegm at the back of one's
tongue. It wasn't flamenco anymore. Messiaen's bird
                                                    books
      rang and rang, flew as if thrown our way... Better
to've let longing last Itamar announced, adjunct in-
struction we sat hammered by. He spoke as a refugee
                                                    from
      thought's own heaven. The endlessness of longing
   it was we were now taught, the small share we get
   of eternity Itamar called it, piano ping riffling his jaw.
"Long on longing, short on time," one wanted to say but
                                                    bit
   one's tongue. Itamar's noetics were no joke... The lights
      flickered off and on in the subway tube it turned out
we were in. Piano ping lingered on Itamar's jaw, peal as
                                                    much
      as ping, pound as much as peal, we sensed we were
      in London but unclear. We saw the city was not eter-
nal nor the subway we were on, the seats we sat in as well.
   The glint of light off the leaves on the trees outside was
                                                    also
      not eternal, something seen in a face face fell away
from likewise, Itamar taught, the waft of his and his lady's
   loin musk not eternal. Nothing was eternal, we were
                                                    fla-
      menco again, Nub's nightmare politics also not eter-
nal, moot condolence or consolation, fleet solace whatever
                                                    sol-
   ace it
was

Itamar knew he was he only insofar, rejuvenant
   spook, rejuvenant spy out of time's own house. His
woman's love part's Proustian bouquet stayed on his
                                                  fin-
   gertips, love's numinosity let linger, let go, rem-
nant stir to which he'd been consigned... Recom-
   binant sound her he she knew, she too only she inso-
far. What it meant was that the thought of what was
                                                  there
   was more there than what was there, what was there
less there when they arrived. Creation, Itamar taught,
   intimated cremation, an alchemico-tantric precept Huff
                                              had
left him with... The day on which it all became clear... All
                                            angst,

   all ambient clench, all
catch

So it went in the dark we were caught in, greed gone
   viral at the top, word gotten out by the blow ghost,
  "Let them die," Legba's limp never more pronounced.
                                     We

    had come to where the subway train split, a long Y
   made by the two ways it went, two vigilances, Itamar's
   book. A willingness not to be were to be to be caught
                                       out

   rode or drove it, so ephemeral a wisp we knew… We
   rayed out between the arms of the Y even so, a widen-
 ing piazza predicated on extremity, cold eternity, that
                                 which
  we would never reach but, undulant, corpuscular, always
                                 be

  beckoned
  by

for Robert Duncan & Peter O'Leary

Greed's faux goodness lorded over us, the
one-third had thrown us to the dogs. In-
to the recesses of love we now went, a new
                                                    word
we made up, "steepage," led the way, the
arrival Itamar's muse intimated loomed un-
reachable, there less there than in thought...
                                                    The
abandoned boy and the abandoned girl fell
into strife our non-arrival announced, fought as
to who stood abandoned more, each in a real
                                                    and
imagined way left out. Might the Golden Ones
be among us again we begged, intervening, be
them or be with them, the abandoned girl, the
                                                    aban-
doned boy. The fight's blue connotation wore
thin the more strongly we begged, prayer's out-
line or limit come upon as upon a magic wand, a
burial mound. Crux and curvature were oddly one
                                                    we
noted, new to their masonic drive... The Golden
Ones roamed occluded but for a glimpse not given
to linger, cloud enough to blot out the sun, cloud all
                                                    over
us. None other than the greed, Brother B avowed
and Anuncia amen'd him, the greed great beyond
words' ability to say, numbers' to tell. "Seep" ran
one with "steepage," a strange brew everything
                                                    more
than our means conjured up. *And there we wept*
torn a new one, sand poured out of our cried-out
eyes. We were all but or about to be dead, density
                                                    our
witness, out into the appurtenances of night... That
the Golden Ones, next to never seen, might be glimpsed,
redolent of coin absconded with, we stepped in... We
                                                    told

them, the abandoned girl, the abandoned boy, they
were not—the greed, Brother B ranted, beyond belief—
we told them, the abandoned girl, the abandoned boy,

we

told them they were not the on-
ly ones

•

We slept inside myth but were stirred by ythm, fur-
tive gold we the bereft ran with. Not that the Golden
Ones, next to never seen, be seen, Anjali, new to our

crew,

pronounced. It was that the haptic take hold of us,
a sense of being run with, auspice we more stayed
inside than saw, stood inside, run though we would

and

though we did... The Golden Ones were gone but
for the beseeching, themselves the beseeching our
best hope. Anjali said as much, raw recruit, new to

our

dismay's reconnoiter, churchical armful Bouadjé
put his arm around while she spoke... She was hope's
main squeeze, hope as hope would have it, hope's
mere mention, the abandoned ones the Golden Ones, at

each

other's throats though they
were

•

Spitless, tongueless mouthing what passed for
  love in the place we were in, bite what had been
kisses, grab took embrace's place, deep into lip-
  lessness we now went. The life whose residue the
                                                   words

  were surrounded us, Nub's new phase too horrid
to be ignored, reminisce the Golden Ones though
  we did... No redemptive narrative paved our way,
                                                no

    matter we had somewhere to go, no matter no
way we'd have said we were lost. It was the every-
  thing everything was, the keeping on kept keeping on.
It would do that until it stopped, as would we. No need
                                               was

  there for summing up... Were the Golden Ones an al-
  chemical conceit Huff's drift of late had us wondering.
A shyster conceit the more skeptical had it, the Huther-
  ing Ones, Nub's new reality show. Kleptocratic switch
                                            gave

  gold a bad name... It wasn't gold we were after, we'd
been there and gone. Nor was it home, we'd been there
as well. Bits of bread marked our way, black bread and
                                            ru-

  bles. "Salt sandwiches" awaited us we'd heard, salt
sanguinity. Neither were we lost nor would they be eaten,
  such the sort of dream we were having, residual steep-
age more than we could know. "Please, please, Dr. D,"
                                              we

found ourselves begging, "bring them back," skeptical
  or not, inured to not knowing, gnostic agnostics in a
pinch... We'd begun eking out the minutes, the hours, the
                                          days,

  our day soon come. We let ourselves linger in the space
between *a-* and *gn-*, the cut we called it, counting out where
                                          no

  numbers
were

I stood witnessing it from afar, bodily breakdown
a language or a lexicon it seemed, hamstring tight
   as a fist, bone gone, the Golden Ones but a body of
                                                lore.
    I stood angry on all fronts, no churchical armful
   beside me, bodily breakdown's prophecy the future
      bore in, Brother B, so grim it got, went biblical,
"The greed giveth not," he proclaimed... The life the
                                        words
    were the residue of receded... It was... It wanted all
      of itself... It awaited... It would begin its redoing,
   could it... It went... It wanted... It was all accents and
                                       flats...

    It waited... It was
only

Out of the gold bell of many a horn, our Golden Ones
   the Crackling Blue Ones, of late between yes and
maybe, no and maybe, maybe and perhaps, a dotted
                                         rest
    among microtones... Gold gave itself over into
  the palms of our hands, not that we renounced it, not
   that we thought it was ours, not that we'd ever not
                                       call
it hard to tell, none of it never be known to be in vain, a
                                       blue,
    shading late-
ness

(slogan)

The Golden Ones, the Crackling Blue Ones,
   wore birds' heads, cracked seeds thrown into
  bells around their necks, the poverty of time

                                 gone
    again into the coin purse, lifted bells we rang

                                      free-
dom from

AHDJA'S TESTAMENT BECOMING CELESTRIAL

—"mu" two hundred twenty-fifth part—

We were nearing the soon-come capital of
New Not Yet. We knew where we were go-
ing, we knew whereof we spoke. We were
                                    soon
to see our circling end. Ahdja said a large
rock had been taken away, the boulder roll-
away bodiliness had been gotten out of our
                                    way,
runaway drift it spawned or itself already
was... We were of a different disposition, she
said, a kind of pilgrim the new confedera-
cy's pillaging set loose. What were roots when
                                    the
ground got stolen she gave us to wonder and
what birthright was place itself. Say what you
will, she said, all of it was God, the confusing
                                    part,
the greed our moment's Golden Ones, we
grew dark enough to say, such things long since
decided at the level of the cell... Was it body
                                    gone
against itself to be more than body, she half-
queried, half-answered, question jamming an-
swer, other than itself if nothing else, rollaway
                                    de-
fault. The trees we gazed out at turned into
sticks as we moved along, late work to be called
pilgrim made apropos, Nub's inevitable stub-
ble foretold. We moved in a kind of shared conva-
lescence, bodily acuity attuned to what ailed
                                    with-
in and without, each athwart the thing that be-
set us we had come to call time, pretending to
name was to know exactly what... The trees we
gazed out at turned into sawed-off stumps of hair,
                                    the
premises' namesake stumps Ahdja said they
were, Nub's late realty show, Nub's new end-

times talk. We each could see parts of our lives

                                          re-

combined and brought back, all of it as it cut our
   heads open, differently permuted no matter or
   exactly the matter, we were wishing we could see

                                       our

   parents now, knowing what we knew. We were
wishing we could tell them what we'd been thru,
   dead though they were, dead though they'd long
since been... The red sky gray, the greed's carapace,

                                 bod-

   ies in decline, we wanted to see siblings, mothers,
   fathers, nieces, uncles, nephews, aunts, unsure
where we were the farther we moved on. It might've
   been Fennario, so far it was from anywhere we'd

                              been,

   but it was Nur, Crater, Tracer, Nub, the backland
of New Not Yet. We were nearing the soon-come
   capital even so, no matter if not exactly the matter,

                           a

   wounded sense of place gotten at again. "Made
to be made to want to holler from birth it seems"
   was Ahdja's new precept. "A congeries of limbs

                        and

   conjoint sweetness," she went on, "the which par-
   taken of, the lay grace of dream." All that had
been done in the name of gold clamored at our feet,

                          Ah-

   dja's faraway harp trinkled in the background, a
   harp whose haunt we dreamt we trod shoeless, the
blabbering dead fallen away someday... It wasn't hers to
say but she said it. It wasn't that when it came to New

                         Not

   Yet we were already there, always there, it wasn't
that. It wasn't that all that had been done in the name of
   gold came into conscience's light, knew itself anew,

                         the

   greedy ones the guilty ones, feeling it for once. It
was the chattering of teeth we heard as the soon-come

                        capi-

   tal drew
near

•

And once we were in the capital of New Not Yet,
soon-come, the icy epithet, melted, toward which,
we knew, our bewilderment leaned. Our heads had

           got-
ten heavier the farther we came, the longer we
carried them, the pragmatics of what came to hand
a fleet elixir, an ether lazing lightly on the air. A

        rock
had been rolled away, Ahdja said. Meaning what, we
wondered, sensing what drift we could, which was-
n't much. We let it lead us, a teased unseizability, thread

      so
thin it cut right thru… Her sweet dream of someone
long lost kept coming up, someone never found it seemed
at points. They had lain naked on a train remembering

     when,
fraught reunion, far-flung legs and arms a snug world
in whose reach, Nub's apprentice prez against all that.
Take me back, the dream's meaning, *Take us back*,
it spoke with two tongues. They were stranded kin come

    up-
on each other as in a storm, all of it auguring bodily mis-
prision, immaterial conjugant the soul of it was, her
insisting only what fed it, telling us nothing if not what

    soul
was… Was it the question or the answer jammed us
New Not Yet's exacted air gave cause to wonder, a con-
centric eccentricity of sorts peeling away what com-
mand there was, the whatness we were ever in whose debt.

   All
would be well it seemed or we at least wanted to say. The
hoodoo Ahdja's dream amounted to made us hopeful, we
the very ones who'd been wary, if not fear for whom a kind

    of
befuddlement had ensued, the parsing of degree, grada-
tion, detour. "I'm listening," we said, each of us, Ahdja's
rollaway spiel a boon, beknownst or not no matter but be-
knownst, the bits of paper falling from the sky nothing if

    not
its announcement, the capital of New Not Yet not unlike
we thought it would be… It was a dream of sweet con-

sent, sex-polis torn a brand new, the legendary land of grab

                                                    gone
    away… We were there. There we were… There we were.
We were there… As though a ditty rode the air making light of
  our dismay, the perplexity of the living preluding the same

                                               such
of the dead, we felt what muscle we had melting away but
  were okay with it, all, we thought, in the goodness of time…
There we were. We were there… We were there, there we

                                             were,
  persuaded by Ahdja's beauty truth would out. We caught
equations between inside and out, trying to think about the
  state, trying to think about economics, money's migration so
many rocks we swallowed, rollaway stone lining our stomachs,

                                             the
  tally of what had been done in the name of gold without num-
ber. Was it we were not really there we wondered, no way not
  to be there, no way not to not be there, not there in name only,

                                          there.
    It was neither here nor there to us whether we solved it, in's
function of out, out's function of in. The question was its an-
  swer, jammed answer, answer jamming question always…
We were deep into what Nub was calling "The Drumpf Show,"

                                          real-
  ty or reality none of them would say. Ahdja said realty and we
  said it too, reality the elsewhere New Not Yet was. So to be in-
sisted, a sense all but something like pastoral came over us, no

                                          be-
  lief but in what-
  if

•

"The lay grace of dream's decree," Ahdja held forth, her-
   self of such grace we blinked and went blind, Ahdja
whose toes we'd have kissed. The perplexity of the living
                                                   her
   theme, the dead perplexed as well, made to want to hol-
ler, she said, we do holler, braced against what's to come.
   "I've been thinking about leaving my body," she said, said
                                                    it,
      as they say, without affect… There was a new tune on
   the box, "Ahdja by Starlight," the offshore horns' recondity
   afoot, deep ourkestral brass at its beck. "Bounty be our
bond," we pled, buttock-struck, bottom-heavy Ahdja a bell
                                                   or
      a pear. We'd have sniffed in between her toes, kissed each
   one, so replete her teaching, men and women both, we
   the alchemico-tantric entourage. "I've been thinking about
                                                   leav-
   ing my body," she said again, cerebral, nonchalant, non-
      plussed, genital splendor, the pelvic tonic the night draped
   her in, less than an afterthought. Stars lay atop our mountainous
   night, stars we instead stood counting… We had carried our
                                                   lives
      in the palms of our hands, little rectangles Wallace Berman-
   style, telephonic intel bane and blessing, we got relief staring
                                                   in-
   to the
sky

It was a night of counting stars, the brows of our faces
    pulled back like windows, blank space we peered out of
emoting against all odds, eyes big as kids' again. We the
                                                        mys-
        tic we we were, no belief but in what-is's would-be
    twin. We were there but only halfway there, if that much,
        immersed as much elsewhere, maybe more. We were
    there, there we were, lest reality lapse into realty, reminded
                                                        none
        of it could we possess, we were the possessed... Starlight
    rode us like lightning. We were the horses of whom it said,
        "Tell my horse." A kind of majesty struck and stuck to us, a
                                                        kind
        of resonance and with it a kind of lushness, wary not to
    be pleased with itself, not to adore its own beauty but be
        lit with it, tangential, somehow, to itself... One's memory
    lingered on the outskirts of New Not Yet, come lately from
                                                        Con-
        niption City to found a faith no one would follow, one all
    one's own... We were each that one, that we, the starlight rode
        us like water, we whose eroded witness ran from New Not
                                                        Yet

        to the
sea

ANUNCIO'S FIFTEENTH LAST LOVE SONG

—"mu" two hundred twenty-sixth part—

Wanted to say, "Long since not seeking Anuncia's
  kiss," wanted to sing it, a last love song again.
  Looked out at the lake pulling back from him, of
                                                late
    in the condition of things but rebuked, looked
      out at snow pocked and mottled by shadows, the
  frozen lake's portation farther out. Wanted to say,
                                                "Only
      to be like ice," a late winter, a lost summer song...
  Wanted to be done with juggling *loquat* and *loqua-*
  cious, what she'd have called fruitlessness. He knelt
  instead sipping toenail soup, flashback, throwback,
                                                had
      sworn he'd kiss Ahdja's feet. She of the dream's
  lay grace again, ply upon ply, each an overlay of oth-
  ers and an underlay, Ahdja some new Anuncia, his
                                                old-
    time never, Nunca, each he'd ever known and some
      not... Wanted to say, "Never to be reminded of Anun-
  cia, she of the long toes, me of the red bowtie, sex what
                                                little
      respite, what remit." Snow turning gray as he looked
  out wanting to sing, semising, semisay, "All I want is
  to be done with getting ready to be done," he wanted
                                                to
      say. It wasn't that Ahdja was or would ever be An-
  jali to his Bouadjé, Anuncia not having been able to
    be. Ahdja's "I've been thinking about leaving my body"
  was what it was, himself begun to be made metaphysical
                                                by
      bodily breakdown, breath, body and bone absconded
        with... Metaphysical wont stirred by Ahdja's rollaway
  talk, her drape of starlight, he wanted to say something
    came over him, say it more than sing it, not semisay, not
                                                sem-
      ising, wanted to say something got to him. But to say
  was to betray, he thought, words' mystic raiment notwith-
    standing, to clothe or try to clothe what wore but itself.
                                                Like-

wise Anuncia's nether kiss, the swearing off of which was
   not the last love song, the swearing off of singing what
                                                                   it
was

                        •

   He wanted not to tell of overghost horns, emitted
      wind blown against carbon exhaust, bomb, bullet,
   not to speak of breath under attack. He wanted not
                                                               to
      speak of late life in the bowels of Nub, love's in-
         terrupted song, news of another outrage, what
   the apprentice prez did Nub's nightly cud. He want-
   ed not to say Nub shut him up or say love shut him
                                                             up...
   He wanted someone to ask about Nub. He wanted to
      answer that Nub had made us all orphans. Nub is
      watching one's beloved fall apart he wanted Anuncia
                                                            to
      say, back from before, when they were still dream-
   ing. He'd awoken barely able to walk, an allegory of
      what, he wondered, was it. He wanted to say later for
                                                              all
      that, bodily decline boding no utopia, later but that
   love will have gone social, the capital of New Not Yet...
      "Light will have lit us up," he wanted to say, "where
                                                           Main
      meets Amen Street." He wanted to write a nonso-
   nant sonnet, to rhyme *ontology* with *oncology*, though
   he knew that would be too much. He'd been think-
   ing about losing his body. He wanted to go the way of
                                                             not-
      say, say without saying, "I've been thinking about
         my steal-away body, Ahdja's float-away feet." The
   gaps between Ahdja's toes were what horizon there
                                                            was,
      ice or the lake's retreat of like order, the unthinkable
   thought of not. Each gap glittered, infinitely starlit, intersti-
   ce's deep recession, Ahdja's hieratic bequest... How to
                                                            sing
      the nonsong, not say, sing his body's decline with-
      out singing, how not to remember Anuncia's wet kisses,

the string of spit from her bottom lip with her on top.
                                                                                He

no longer lay busted up but walked with back, shoul-
    ders and legs hurting, his body a pain machine, the it of
it upon him, physical, "meta-" merely a wish... Mind's

                                                                    mat-

    ter no matter, he thought, but Fela came on the box
wearing a bone suit, body's contrabass complaint. What
    to say or not say when it turns on itself, he wanted to

                                                                    ask,

    wants not to be it-
self

The apprentice prez had said, "Some of who you
backed," meaning "Whom some of you backed."
Not-say, Anuncio knew, cut many ways. He was

                                               want-
   ing not to ask about slave equity, not to talk a-
 bout getting paid. He wanted not to say, "In but not
  of the body," not to sing or say, "In but not of the
                                              world."
No angel of illness would he speak of, no song of the
   dying earth his to sing, no song of the dearth of love,
  no piled upon no... But the Crusaders came on the
                                          box,
   "Freedom Song," made a march of the moment,
 march though it may not have been. He was in the realm
 of qualities, no measure for which was there. Only the
                                           not

  almost got
close

                            •

The sun sat suspended in blue, snow mostly gone,
here and there a mound of it remained in the shade.
Thus the clarity of the day as it first occurred to him
                                                    a-
    gain, having to part with the world, seeing it as all
façade, a gruff teddy bear he turned out to be. Prophe-
cy sounded different now, sweet corn a god's ear
                                        ren-
    dered up all it was, the great gettin'-up dawn we
get out of the world, ushering horns the awaited
    arms around our shoulders as we go out... "Take
                                        your
    time," he heard someone say, time taken griev-
ance enough, he thought, to be so comforted gave him
    pause. "Take your time," the same someone said
again. "Say it again," yet another someone said. He bit
                                                the
    insides of his lips, parsing the last love song he sang
    or would-be sang, the last love song he not-sang.
"Take your time," the same someone said for the third
                                                time.
"Say it again," the other someone said again. All one to
    him whether he sang or not-sang it seemed or so he in-
sisted, all one whether Anuncia's tossed rump reached
                                        him
    or not, quaint vessel he took body to be... Thus it went
among Anuncio's not-congregants, a sheer feeling in the air
    they turned out to be. He took his time. Banana leaves
                                        caught
    in the wind couldn't have said more... "Tell it like it
is," they were now saying, "Tell it like it is," this and the
                                        other
    someone
    both

The realty show continued unabated. We the uprooted
   wandered on. We got away from Nub and from Anun-
cio's consternation, the antiphonal chorus the not-song
                                        im-

   plicitly summoned, explicit notwithstanding we
  were. We sang our hypothetical hearts out, *is* to his *is-*
not, disburse to his *disavow,* a taste for contradiction
                                     on
  our teeth and tongues… Anuncia let her dress's drape
   fall from her hips in the refrain we kept coming to,
dream or no dream though he demanded we say outright,
                                  Ahdja's

  rollaway night if
not

Ahdja stood concentric with Anuncia, Anuncia concen-
tric with her, an out-of-his-head raving Anuncio's
last love song bordered on. What Nub had to do with it
                                                    flick-
    ered, there but not all there, backdrop that wouldn't
go away… Nub's coloration clouded itself, white as
    it would-be was. "Drunken boat" he heard as "bloated
vote," lifting words for his would-be sonnet, fickle sonnet
                                                    more
    so than be-
fore

We the uprooted wandered on, the unreal estate
  we were relegated to. Was it we's romance,
over time, wasn't enough we scratched our heads
                                 won-

  dering, scratched our synaptic circuitry, all but
ripped it out it seemed. Was it the other, over time,
  drew romance's rebuke we the uprooted stood
                               ask-

  ing, throats raw, phlegm tamping down our
tongues… "On these we stand," we'd have said
  had it been poetry. We'd have said, "This is our
music," had it been music. What to say, what to
                               say,
  we pounded the heels of our hands together ask-
ing, the hypothetical chorus we'd become at
  a loss for words. "An affront to love," we said at
                               last,

  speaking of polis, all but cliché we could see
but it fit, Nub's ongoing disgrace… We thought may-
  be it must've been music, the escorting horns at our
                               backs

  again, a long, slow, drawn-out waltz. A trumpet
stood out, so looted for sound we almost wept, it was
  taps it played we could've sworn. It made a case
against the piano's right-hand chime but complied as
                               well,
  toll nothing it would have to do with but did, toll-
  ing for all who heard and who didn't hear. We
thought maybe it must've been the offshore horns, a
  sad fanfare if not taps. "Never all there," they kept
                               re-

  peating or those were the words we put in their
mouths. We the uprooted went on wandering, tongue
  tip and lip a kind of meat we let sweeten, true to
                               our
  bodily wood's recruitment, we soldiered on as the
  horns blew. It was the soul's night out, nothing less,
no "post-," ourselves ransacked for sound… It wasn't
                               we
  didn't all know what was coming. We looked loving-

ly at our watches knowing the dead don't wear them,
we were still alive. We were way past the Chattahoo-
chee, we came to many an anonymous river that more

                                than

    speaking spoke dialect, a thick slang we got mud all
over us from… A new condition it was we'd come to
    Anuncio proclaimed, come to or been come to by, con-
ditionality itself, he went so far as to say, a "baptismal

                            hap-

    ticity" he called it. Another last love song welled up
for the singing, he told us, punning, a *last* as in *last-
ing* he played and put his hopes on, no song his last

                          but

    lasting. So it seemed to him at least, he whose head,
    rollaway horn, blown-over hollow, we'd gone inside…
Otherwise we heard ducks not far away, a symphony of

                        elat-

    ed complaint. This was a place we will have been while
alive it seemed it said, seeming say we cocked our ears
    to hear more clearly. What say lay below the quacking lay

                        so

    deep it hurt, seeming say's eschatological way with us
wielded like a hook. What to say, what to say, we were
    pounding the heels of our hands together asking, say taken
down so deeply, say turned in on itself. Not since Quag had

                        we

    felt so bereft, Nub's reversion to its worst a daily attack,
    the comb-over coup. We patted the heels of our hands
together, something we'd heard Muddy sing about, patted,

                        what

    to say, what to
do

We carried it in our heads, the boughs, the leaves,
   the needles, the carpeted forest floor, ourselves
  escorted out, antlers they might've been. The long
                                              song
  preceded us, out from inside, asking what but traps
bodies were. There was never a bent note not heaven's
  arrow, never not the pitch of it, down though it slid,
                                                 an
inconsequent phlegm the waning of romance Anun-
  cio sang… A kind of contagion it'd been but it
  relented, Anuncio's confounding of Anuncia with
                                          Ahdja,
  the two-headed mambo they'd been. What loomed
and lay upon us cut differently, a coming something
  that would not be Nub, not New Not Yet, loomed and
                                        oth-
erwise lay upon us. We were tramping to make heaven
  home, home heaven, the bent notes' testament the
word we went by, a kind of refuge in the elsewhere they
                                        were,

  pilgrims of sorrow we
were

•

We carried it in our heads, the boughs, the leaves,
   the needles, the carpeted forest floor, ourselves
   escorted out, antlers they might've been. The long

                                 song
   preceded us, out from inside, asking what but traps
bodies were. There was never a bent note not heaven's
   arrow, never not the pitch of it, down though it slid,

                                  an
inconsequent phlegm the waning of romance Anun-
   cio sang... A kind of contagion it'd been but it
   relented, Anuncio's confounding of Anuncia with

                              Ahdja,
   the two-headed mambo they'd been. He was be-
  yond all that now, he said, love's or song's last-
   ness or lastingness, no sooner said than we rode with

                                  it,
   something seen in a face, something subject to hold,
   have, grabbed at, gone... What loomed and lay upon
us cut differently, a coming something that would not

                                be
   Nub, not New Not Yet, loomed and otherwise lay
upon us. We were tramping to make heaven home,
   home heaven, the bent notes' testament the word we

                                went
by, a kind of refuge in the elsewhere they were, pilgrims
   of sorrow we were... Anuncia, we found out, had said,
   "Let's die now," resonant of Nub's national romance,

                            Ah-
dja's thought of leaving her body, the end of the world
   more likely than decapitism's end, thanatologic after-
   glow. Phlegm sequed into pilgrim, a logic recondite

                              but
   for the sound or the face of it, some something at
the loin level grabbed like property, Nub's necropolitan
   advance a pall over all of us, what-to-say's incum-
bent rebuff... We were dreaming it all would have been

                              only
   a bad dream when we awoke, away from exactly which
we were off like fugitives, love's prolongation the point of

                              our

   run

There was an inward pearl, a certain inward pearl we
made what went on outside pay. A seeming so, a cer-
tain say, deep into *The Book of So* we went, this was

                                            our
   journey now… Set out to pry so from seeming, the
book we made being there from making book on be-
  ing there, no bet would accrue to guessing this or that.
                                             All
 had been thrown up for grabs otherwise, thus exactly it
   was. We heard it receding, oud-lit hearth and hollow
that would not be come abreast of again… We came up
                                      with
   answers, what to say, what to do… We wept without
  water to cry with. Harps of David hung from trees, bending
                                      the
boughs

We had the news on the tol'you, no music on the box,
   supping our daily fare of abuse. Annals of the Udhrite
school repurposed, we were those who when watching
                                                      die.
      Talk of a tax plan, the Klan, Russia, another school
         shooting. We were leaving sooner or later, said the an-
chor, face too large for his head, said without saying it
   it seemed… The cooks in the kitchen wore baseball caps,
                                                         went
on cooking, their message was we'd get by. They were
   auguring exit from the world of difference, indifferent,
                                                      ada-
      mant, unbeknownst or
      not

IV
PILGRIM

SAID BOOK SAID TO HAVE BEEN

—"mu" two hundred twenty-eighth part—

A baroque swell had us wayward. We
 were living lives not knowing what.
What-to-say and what-to-do's incessant
                                        harp-
     ing yielded finitude. We laughed re-
naming ourselves the blessed of the earth.
 It was a turn we ourselves knew better
                                        than,
     not the tribe's way anymore, the be-
 ing-we, upstrung emollience apocryphal
    at best, annals of a won't-be we… We
                                        had
given up on the world, decided elsewhere
    was where we were from. Sun Ra's old-time
Saturn we were headed for, a name whose
                                        repe-
     tition offered solace, now that the guns
 were out. Parkland the new Sandy Hook,
   Parkland the new Columbine, Nub's new
spelling NRA, Nar we called it now. Ran
                                        we
    also called it, running, no out as yet… I
    wanted to say all had reared up to the eye
 and to the soul as though there for the last
                                        time.
    Some of that, though, had been taken, we
  on our preemptive pilgrimage caught out,
    a rush of raw thought everywhere at once.
                                        A
Brazil of the mind intervened, Jair such body
   and sweat we sought respite, a drunken flight
passed out on once on the way to São Paulo,
                                        not
    that Nub wasn't there as well… Not that the
      thin road we walked meant more than the
strait it portended, upstart exit some said would
 get us hurt, heart's leave or elation, all nonce
                                        ex-

empla. We were deep into Tête's world of wor-
      ry, we were out on the rolling sea on dry land...
Someone said pilgrim again and I said yes. A
                                        re-
      membrance, a reconnoiter, a certain clime it
all came to. A baroque swell had us wayward,
      a rogue sough or insistence held us up or hauled
                                                   us
      in

•

Not so much we as a migrating they, we the
migrating they, exotic to ourselves the instant
 we gave it thought, a tapering strait we alighted
from. We the migrating they were Bauls of Outer
                                        Pra-
  desh, the Hammond B-3 our harmonium, Tête's
   roil a nervousness on high. What-to-say-what-to-
do rubbed us raw, an eastward-leaning draw we
                                        rode
  not announcing ourselves, the migrating they we
were yet to've embarked or to be booked, such book
as there was only said to've been… We were they
                                        be-
  fore we knew it, themselves by default, vagabond
   ambit we moved in whose pursuit, proximity's
kingdom come. To be there was to weather asymptote
regard, say ourselves raw, whatsay's heaven our
                                        heads
   pivoting nigh, nearness's kiss pure dissolve. At-
mospheric remit was all we could call it, call having
   come to a diffuseness nearness knew. "Yes, I'm
                                        the
one," one wanted to say, thumping one's chest, old-
  school assurance by and by not yet come… More
days went by. We were on whatness alert. We lay low
                                        be-
  hind sandbags awaiting the next wave, alive but so
   far from Low Forest, home an old word we almost
knew but had long ago lost, home was a word we'd
heard… Sonic reprisal sought us out it appeared, the
                                        blos-
  som inside death, the sense of a journey had retreat-
ed some. So much to mourn, so much to make what
of it we could, our heads' fragility the caravan thru a
                                        nee-
  dle's eye it seemed or it was, that or such else it over-
took us, turned us around, as though a book floated up
from the hand that had been holding it, up and into the
                                        air

   as if on its
own

•

What kept calling us back was we were the ones
who set it up, no trace of it otherwise. It was what
  made the trek or the trip we were on. Sound which
                                                    had
    been on our side no longer was. Autonomic sound
  named itself anew. All the ways other than we were
    we could've been gnawed at us now, Nub now a place
                                                    ap-
    portioning hell, Nub long such a place… We stole away
      to reflect, Netsanet and I-Insofar, flesh to be taken for
granted, bone to be foregone. Medicine coated our tongues
                                                            no
    matter we kissed, a comestible book like the one John
      swallowed, our kiss and our coated tongues that book.
                                                        We
    leaned in scatting the book, said book such as it was, lost
      in everlasting whatness… Book, we bartered, go if not be
                                                        our
  bond

So it will be, I thought and said, and so it was.
　　Our medicine tongues wagged unobstructed, say
so irrelevant everyone thought. I-Insofar's mirror
　　　　　　　　　　　　　　　　　twin
　　spoke of beauty's baitless hook, something seen
　　in a face he now gave up on, live-and-let-live
no state's pursuit... So sad a note to go out on, I
　　thought, hip lost, knee buckling, a screw loose in
　　　　　　　　　　　　　　　　polis's
　　head, kleptocratic scheme number no one knew
　　which come to light... But the book of say no sooner
　　spoke than faded, felt throughout all the premises,
　　　　　　　　　　　　　　　　　the
　　book of see said also to've
gone

Body and bone's metaphysical wish was
upon us again, Andreannette long since its
  avatar, she herself so put upon..We pushed
                                   off
against a continent that seemed only a curb,
  continent's edge our perennial pivot, the
  launch point we knew as Lone Coast... Lone
                                  bodi-
  liness and bone we meant to say of it, stood
as we did as veritable salt crashed in, a token
  to be taken away we knew. Netsanet and I
slipped away again, took each between our lips
                                  the
  other's tongue, the intoxicant spit was again,
    tej, again, it might've been and was... We
lay like pilgrims in the sand on Seabright Beach,
                                sand
  a golden honey we'd have sworn, our tongues'
    tej's influence, tej's bet. A kind of research,
a kind of resurgence, a kind of talk the mere thought
  of which meant arousal, recursion, wrack. We lay
                                in
  what bordered on wallow, a certain sorrow it all
would pass and with what but bodies to do what
  with, but what would pass to address it with. We
                                lay
in the sand, a sacred spot, being sacred us pilgrim-
  ing there, seaweed and merperson smells our new
                                unc-
  tion, new and old unction
again

     •

Falling away fell away. The cliffs, the erosion, the
  coast. Ice plants gathered more dust. Time had
  moved without us we could feel, the one physical
                              war-
  rant we knew. Horns enticed us leeward, strings
escorted us back... Scared sexless, we lay like lambs,

death soon come it seemed. "There comes a time

to

testify," Netsanet said, standing up, brushing off
the sand we'd lain in loin-to-loin forty-some years
before, night's coat of stars what blanket we had…

She

dug a hole in the sand and poured champagne in.
She put a clump of green grapes on a plate at
its edge. Soon say fell away from all that mattered,

sing-

ing wood took hold of our tongues and our lips. She
traced Ethiopian lines in the sand… Lines were only
crossed eyes it seemed or she made it seem, sight line

of

late low as her low bosom, she of the heavy frame
the froth in from out laid claim to, Netsanet the Beauti-
ful One again said to've come. There but not there
but seeming so, stolid so doing, Netsanet late of the fog's

roll

in, Netsanet, I said, my steal-away one… Time so
whisking us away we could feel it, Run beginning to be
like Urn, Nur like Urn, the deep wound mortality was

was

what was in a
name

We had lain imagining an art of absolution, a pro-
    positional art making its point as it staggered
back. Some spirit's report a hand other than ours
                                                    put
    there would regale us, each as if a ghost back
        for one more 'gain… The greed, Brother B had
preached, put a pall on everything. We were in
    Our Lady of the Bay Leaf's house no matter, the
                                                    men-
    tion of whose name sponged our brows with vin-
egar, now that we were immigrants again. Honey
    turned into grains of sand that were almost amber,
                                                    yel-
    low with what but sex to know respite, gold but with
                                                    not
    even
    that

•

(chant)

We stood imagining we were leading a new
band, the Onshore Reed Optet, imagining what
one saw was what one got. The day, back to
                                                being
   day, called up song number five to the third
times two, song number ten to the third divided
by five. Right away we hit. A sublimate of
                                                gold
coated our instruments, a sulfide or a caliphate,
   an algorithmic stutter, song number five hun-
dred divided by two... The song sang itself, tallied
                                                its
   name, its number, a temporizing tack we listed
with. It kept locating itself, locating us. We were
way beyond lost otherwise, deeply perdido, dream
                                                with-
   in a dream of having gone. What it was was we
were trying to keep our heads on, Netsanet's thrown
   she averred, mine as well, our thrown heads gone
but for that... As though we bent pipe to fit recondite
                                                spa-
   ces, copper pipe, we played, awake with only one
eye open, dreaming. We were trying to contain
what contained us, history we'd heard it called. All
                                                the
   one in three gave the grabber weighed heavy. We
would all go up in vapor we dreamt, dreaded. We
   played, awake with one eye closed... I was aware
                                                of
her nether mouth's remit were one so favored, the
   fact it lay there, collateral, nonchalant. We were be-
ing worn off on by a book we'd read, a book we 'd
                                                seen
   ourselves in, Optet that we were, a book of alchemi-
co-tantric waft, acoustico-tantric, a stale but leaved
   mustiness remote but right up on us, calming, could
                                                it
   be calmed, our complaint. We lamented the hair-
line we live on. We got to where, imagine no mat-

ter we would, we couldn't hear ourselves. An altar-
beach ritual it was, an altercation, the leaves of the

                                             mus-
ty book at our noses like feathers, we whose togeth-
   erness's tokens they'd be… But we saw what we
couldn't hear, heard what we couldn't say, the pall it

                                              all
   came down to and the pull of it, musty inurement,
musty recess. We sniffed what lay too deep to be
   reckoned, plumb auspice "mu" might've been, the

                                          ab-
conded-with book of between. It made us ponder what
   got old and what not, a certain scale we would un-
temper, tamper with, a seashell's report put up to one's

                                          ear…
   A skeletal allegory had hold of us we saw or we heard
   it said, bone musk native to the book, blunt proffer,
sand our hiding place while all eyes watched. Fibrotic ham-
strings tripped us up, no capoeira. The one-third waited

                                          be-
   hind sandbags, the ones whose targets we were. No
matter, no matter, we not so much uttered as knew, gno-
   mic foreboding at our backs we got used to, we the

                                          steal-
away ones, we the steal-away two, thrown heads horse-
   hoofed, horses getaway quick, Netsanet's hurry-up
shunt… We stood hip to hip, elbow to elbow, warding

                                          off
   death it felt like, the Optet no less than the pack we'd

                                        have
   run with, adrift in ceremo-
nial Nur

There was no Netsanet my doctor said. Netsanet's
the name of my fever, I said, the ruse my infir-
mity wore, rough threading. Our forebears had been

                                                   slubs,
   called slubs, a new game when decapitism had
  barely begun... I'd gotten to be at home with the idea
  of adjournment, a journey so often put differently,

                                          ten-
   uous bodies' metaphysical wont. A trip-stepped An-
  dalusian cloud song brought it all out, hitch polished by

                                          rub

    an aspect
  of rub

•

Neither dream nor sleep the problem, awaken-
   ing, being awake, not so. Sex lay lapislike
under the ground we walked like water, a sloped
                                   or

   incipient waning all I knew. Andreannette's
oxymoronic biscuit. Netsanet's talisman. Each as
   of Our Lady of the Wounded Voice whose
                                there-
ness beckoned, amends whose fractal remand
   we would parse, parlay... Bit ecstasy. Mystic re-
mit. Ritual command we fell short of assuming,
                             tiny
   calculi scorched our feet. An alchemico-tantric
fractality. A dividend whose recoil we would al-
   lay. Ritual amends, remembering what it had been
                           to

   be slubs, another mark we ventured shy of as-
suming, naked under it all after all. Meanwhile
   the circus raged outside us, a kleptocratic sublime,
we thought, the way the news went on swooning...
                           "Fun"

   was a word we heard, "fascinating" we heard as
   well, outrage one with thrall in the barker's realm,
the apprentice prez's legerdemain. Meanwhile the
   slaughters went on, too much coin in for them not
                             to,
   decapitism's logic no sense, all our heads lost, all
what we were calling atrocity, inveigh though we did,
   skeletal allegory run dry... "Measure me, measure
                         me,"
the gullet Brother B warned about cried out, "Meas-
   ure me, measure me," laughing us away... We stood a-
thwart kingdoms buried under the sand, where we went
                             when

   we closed our
   eyes

The away place we'd otherwise been or been
    wanting to be, I wanted there to be one, I
wanted it to be, I wanted there to be an away...
    My shoulder clicked announcing that place, one
                                                    such
    place, the closer walk I thought so much about,
        my knees clicked, ligaments and bones jostling, to
                                                    what
    end damn if I
knew

WHAT THE MATTER WAS

—"mu" two hundred thirtieth part—

Came in asking what the matter with time
   was, the dead and the ordeals of the dead
  commemorated, came in commiserated
                          with.
  Had found our way back to the elders,
to we not being the elders, came in wafting
  cinnamon, cilantro, cumin, a crankshaft
                        rode
   us wayward, a chimney made us think.
  Preponderant whimsy, preponderant would...
  Came in, called it a feel thing, said it was
                      noth-
ing but. Bantu bones and Bantu relics crowd-
  ed Valongo. It was again we were in Brazil,
  people of a book yet to be read, our being
                    there
   turned into a book, preemptive elegy may-
be all it was. The matter with time was all
  the falling away, the offshoot way of it, it-
self not itself as such but by sublime illogic,
                   such-
  ness not even itself... "Mu" might've been
  what it was, what the matter was, the name of
it if not, "Mu" might've been having no home
                  but
  setting out, what the matter was having no
  home but setting out. Our being there turned in-
  to a book, an ache no foreknowledge could
                 al-
  lay, knowing no way enough knowing. A
 tint of sorrow subsumed it all, the beckoning
  horns as much holding us up as urging us
on. Riveted, we stood watch it seemed. "Watch
                out,"
  what the matter was warned out loud... Some
   plea was being made, some appeal to reason...
Implicative sanity. Implicative good sense... What
  to say, what to say, the implicative quandary
                sur-

faced again, never not so near its breath lay
on us like drapery, drapery lay on us like
dread. Antique resolve was of no use now, no

                       mat-
ter once having to do with rhyme, recurrence,
no matter "Mu" could mean so much. I heard
Itamar musing to my right, a long since heard

                    be-
fore admonition... "I'm intrigued," he said,
"by churchical girth, an anti-Udhrite school of
embrace and of embouchure, elation allied with
complaint concerning how quaint to be in a body

                      can
be." I told him he fooled himself and that Nur
made us metaphysical, his wish was to be bodi-
less, bulletproof. I spoke from a yet-to-be-arrived-
at perch. I sat strange to myself, dispatched. A

                  B-3
sotto voce scream left my lips. An offshore fra-
cas the horns intimated concurred, ever the unease
the truth of it, the fallen-away "Mu's" remand.

                  Each
wave rolled in like a summons, an invitation, an

                    over-
due debt

•

I cut my teeth on Lone Coast and there we
    were, back. Blue strut, blue straw, blue lachry-
mose moon, a blue star beside it. We'd been

                                    busy
    trying to reason with God. Arms away from
our sides, palms up, an acoustico-metallic traipse
    we lost our way on… It wasn't that we wanted

                                    to,
ever that we wanted to, we wanted to be any-
    thing but blue. Ever the matter what the mat-
ter was, Itamar alchemy's darling no less, an

                                    im-
    plicate art we parsed and would ply, God's
    own implicate wish. We felt bled into by an
alternate book. "Altar," we thought, making

                                    play
    of it. "Host," our newest member put in, a
certain something he'd always been saying he
    said. Ndjaye he said his name was… "I'm just
with you," he went on to say, "not one of you."

                                    His
    independence, we saw, was all in his mouth and
        we passed over it, passed it over. Planting a seed
inside churchical girth, we saw, was, as it was also
    Itamar's and mine, his dearest intent, disavow it no

                                    mat-
    ter we had or we would. The alternate book or the
ultimate book bleeding into us was the what of it,
    the what that was the matter, metaphysicals though

                                    we
    were, the more we
were

•

"Blue Star" was on the box again, Hawk's gra-
   vel part plea, part appraisal, the book we were
bled into by his. His for but a few choruses we
                                                      soon
   found out, Benny's disquisition quick to fol-
low. It was the one in which he reasoned with
   God or with a ghost, the book braiding voices
                                                      not
   only Hawk's, not only his, the one whereby
we reasoned, following him... A tug of war,
   not a pendulum, Benny intimated politics was.
                                                      Be
strong, abide, it seemed he said. Nur would fall
   were we to be as the music was, bent on do-
ing that as we already were, we took it to mean.
                                                      Blue
   swoon. Blue lagoon soon gone. We understood
fanfare now... We knew now what the propor-
   tions were, knew gold to be the complement of
blue. We heard altar construed as attar, churchical
                                                      girth,
   loined anointment, gruff perfume. Thought con-
jured rubbed adjacency, coition's unjointed loins.
   Ndjaye looked on with a grin. We heard a bent note
                                                      rend-
   er host hostage, loined anointment fall away, all
in our minds... The question came up again were
   we ready for star time, ready, Ndjaye slipped in, for
                                                      love's
   low Egyptian beard, a jester in the Pharaoh's house.
   Were we ready for no one thing ever after, he taunted,
likewise Nur, likewise Crater, said no matter what the
                                                      name
   was he knew what we'd say, what our answer was.
He was with us, not one of us, he said... He talked about
   "Sam Cooke's Bobby Womack thing" and we agreed
                                                      he
   wasn't, the night getting sloppy
and big

All along we'd been reasoning with a ghost
  it turned out, trying to reason, reason bor-
dering on plea. As much abraded as bled into
                       by
  the book we were bled into by, damn if we
    knew why the guest would evict its host... The
book bleeding into us the antimatter the matter
  was, a cell turned against its own body, host bid
                      good-
  bye by its guest. As though a house broke itself
apart, brick by anti-brick brick... Something seen
  in a face face was no coming forth from, the river's
                      invi-
  tation turned oneiric the bed
  we were
in

•

(tarry)

We slipped our hands under our dresses
and pants and confected ourselves, any
   angst, any inhibition gone. It was getting
                                             to
   be that time we not only acknowledged
but announced, each a more remote nom-
   ination, the feel thing we'd been told it all
                                             was
more bluntly so... We rode anointing it the
   barren sublime, a flat featureless expanse we
   ground our nubs on, flatness running away, a
                                             flat
   spread of earth all around. We were on the
80, east, heading toward Chicago, Andreannette's
   womanly bravura again on my mind, her ex's
                                             pea-
   coat no matter. We brandished our hands
and held a finger up to each other's nose, deep
   in the hold of the moment, the moment's re-
mainder again, each musing the muse's fecund
                                             re-
cess, a kind of abstention, frank about it, rank
   with it, raw... A practiced entanglement it was,
a tenor saxophone on the box, the saxophonist a
                                             fool
   for love, the horn, barely reined in, seemed in-
tent on biting, a danger to us and to itself. It put us
   all in that frame and made us confess, penitents
                                             in
   the Fool-for-Love Church, a churchical duress
not to be left or made light of. Churchical girth en-
   closed my head like a turban, Andreannette's
umbilic largesse. Her black saint I'd be, the two of
                                             us
   abed in black sheets, black satin, satanic accents
      never not near. What was at issue remained what
the matter was, the what of it the was of it, blur be-
   yond cap or compare... What the matter was was
                                             want-

ing it to add up, to be song number twelve times
twenty-one minus one, song number six times forty-two
   minus one, six to the second times seven minus one,
                                                          tag

to what before was all wont, whence, whither, an in-
   viible song underneath it met up with. Concourse
   with the dead was what the matter was, a dream that
                                                          cut

   water with salt, made us cry. What was the matter
was tally shadowed tarry, would-be rally, wish. What
   was the matter was polis's logic's illogic blew up
                                            a-
gain, the apprentice prez's trigger finger pointed at
   Syria, North Korea, Iran. Wanting not to be but
   could we be music was what was the matter. What
                                                     was

   the matter was it wanted to be subsequence, mo-
ment and moment's afterage, a new word for itself…
   What the matter was was my brother's heart failing,
                                                       Ce-

   cil gone two weeks ago, Wilson before that. What
was the matter was funeral beer sipped lamenting our
   lost body, our lost body being only a number and
                                                     an

   onliness a one-way
pass

Again we were reasoning with God by way
  of a ghost we called holy. I was dream-
  ing, as we all were, women and men both,
                                        all
  of us dreaming of Andreannette. So splen-
did her plenitude was I was back in love's
gallery, a Wrack Tavern reveler again, again
                                  get-
  ting ready to be gone… Everyone was leav-
ing it seemed, last call. I lay on my back in-
side my suspect body. They had cut my leg,
they said, to save it, they had burned my hip,
                                  leg
  all but in a cast, keeping on kept keeping on.
  We abided in truth but for levity's respite
albeit levity abided as well, a new muse and a
                                 new
  ythmology, I lay on my back looking up An-
dreannette's dress… We were drinkers, all of
us drunk, the fools it took to learn. A sad gig
                                  it
turned out to be, our good luck only not to've
  been gunned down yet. Who knew, we won-
dered, what outburst lay in wait. I lay on my
                                back
  inside my suspect body. I lay on my back
torn in two, Mr. Is and Mr. Ain't, beset by the
ghost who was God's proxy, a partridge's call
between… We had been weeping in waltz time,
                                as
  deep as could be in our cups, the misery mu-
  sic was was all ours, such wont as it stirred up
not to be placated. Andreannette stood apart, a
Sophic imposter Sophia said, pitiably wanting
                                to
  highlight or hold on to what went by so fast
we all winced. She of the Chivalric Pea Coat she
called her, lapse the like of antique legend. I
                              saw
her hand move up Andreannette's thigh as last

call, a kind of curtain, came down... So again we
were off and going, stalled in midstep, caught in
                                    Zeno's

    paradox, a premise what we were calling life.
Sophia played God to Andreannette's ghost as we
    ventured one half step and yet another, the heark-
ening of the dead a signpost of sorts, a kind of grrr,
                                                    a

kind of knee-buckle whose arrest we were, all of
    a piece with Nur. Andreannette stood apart feed-
ing us our lines, her tongue-anointed fingertip our
                                            ba-

    ton. A fragrant accord I called it or I thought of
it as, the exact whisk and waft of a kiss the wand
    it was, happenstantial conduction toward no one
knew what... No clock ticked in the tavern. I lay on
                                            my

    back, the underness of Andreannette's dress rare
        air, a helical regard and a kind of transport the way
the Sophic hand found its way up her leg, as though
    all knowledge, all gnosis, resided there. All sport and
                                                    all

        serendipity it also was, nestedness where Andrean-
    nette's legs met, where tryst and trust would rendezvous,
    as well the truth of whose abidance we'd read... Not
                                                    since

Helen had Sophic imposture appeared so real Sophia
    complained, she herself trapped, entranced. Sophic en-
trapment made us all its initiates, a cult whose apostles
                                                    we

    were. To lie on my back was to abide in truth I decid-
        ed. The Temple of Abidance in Truth I cut my teeth
    on lay back on Lone Coast. A hill to my right I turned up
                                                    on-

    to led me
there

It wasn't that nothing ever was anyway but that
  mostly what there was was a name, Andreannette
the wise one, Andreannette the wanted one, the

                                          one
  whose keep, her book said, "abideth." Andre-
    annette it was whose book bore kisses, the wet
of which knew no end, Andreannette of the chur-
  chical girth, earth angel, we her true corps, liege

                                    and
    lief... Andreannette inside whose basilica we
  sat in the nosebleed seats, she was God or a ghost
  whose logic teased us, whose blue star lit our

                                 lips,
  blessed and wet them... "Andreannette" itself,
    the name itself, such an imbuement, the what of

                             what
  was in a
name

•

So much of it was rerun, running backwards, na-
   tion's day done but invited back, likewise ra-
ce's, Nub's new remonstrance, Nur, hope for the
                                          hope-
   less. We the hopeful moved otherwise, the
somewhere we were or were going nowhere we'd
   been, "The Uses of the Real" the name of the
                                          chap-
   ter we came to now. "Would it were 'ruses,'"
   Andreannette lamented and exhaled, almost a
sigh. "Let us be we of a book yet to be written,
                                          re-
sisting the binding of the book. Beware mere
sleight of hand…" The metaphysical we wandered
   on, an echo, a shell. "Bernadette," I recollected
                                          now,
   had been on the box, the Four Tops, a sound
whose catch we were, as with Netsanet but more…
   Something sexual transmigrated it seemed, An-
dreannette our dreams' incessant witness. A mental
                                          field
   it amounted to, winged and ruminant, our regard
   a kind of earthbound shimmer, halo'd exoscopy, the
bending away, it seemed, of all we saw. Mantric was
                                          may-
   be the word for what it was, a mantra taken over
to the eye, no way would the metaphysical we think it
                                          that
   way no mat-
   ter

———————————

Andreannette's bookish ways belied her caveat.
　　She wore horn-rimmed glasses, her mouth big
　with teeth, her ex's pea coat the beginning of
　　　　　　　　　　　　　　　　　　　　wis-
　　dom she said. Her smile invited thought's own
　heaven it appeared... The rest of us wore white
　coats lamenting the shutting down of the lab, a
　　　　　　　　　　　　　　　　　　　　readi-
　　ness whose metaphor it was. A certain waft
　was all we knew of alchemical tantra, sexual wet-
　ness's wound-up air... Time's golden run came
　　　　　　　　　　　　　　　　　　　　as
　news to us, chronophobic so long a part of how
　　we were, our house built ragwise we thought, our
　eventual house, time's golden run partial to no one
　　　　　　　　　　　　　　　　　　　　we

　　thought

(28.iv.18: toll)

 Thus it was one came to be at large in the Take-
Your-Time Church, time not on our side though
 we knew. Momentary crux an evanescent beauty

              so

  honed it made us cry, an apt irrelevance we'd
  have otherwise wanted we now got… We wept
   that it was only for a time, not for all time, we the
metaphysical we, was's redemption we thought, an

              off-

 ness off exactly
enough

(29.iv.18: tally)

Andreannette's bookish good looks had us go-
    ing, thumb out though she'd been on the side of
the highway the day she joined our crew. The
                              road-
    side hallowed by accident, an altar her body
      might've been. God or a ghost, none of us
knew which… Andreannette found it an outrage,
    no matter we took to being scolded, took what
                                light

    could not be made
of lightly

WHAT THE MATTER WAS AGAIN

—"mu" two hundred thirty-second part—

Dawn caught us unawares, another day
  but no new day, another lost cause let go.
We were no longer the people we'd met,
                     the
  they whose we migrated. Our somnial
sway under Andreannette's aegis melt-
  ed away, another awakening to bodily
                 com-
  plaint. What but bodily abidance went
on we'd find out now, trying to make heav-
  en home, home heaven. Were we to be
               doc-
tors, were we to live death ahead of time,
  discontent a ghost or a god in us, god-
liness a bone-chested ghost... Were we to
            be-
  grudge it a whiff of the mystic we fell a-
    way wondering, a heaviness put upon us
we were told we'd wake up from. All in the
  realm of whatsay, sortilege, the air, all that
            was
  in it, on the attack. There was nothing not
caught in crosshairs, metal and smoke was
  our domain. The abandoned girl was among
           us
  again, there was no most or more to be
had... The Not-To-Be-Forgotten Safronia
  she said her name was, redolent of saffron
incense, the closer walk we so wanted and
           so
  long had heard sung about, arms around
each other's waist. She made it all feel nested
  for once, a moment so drunk on nestedness
           we
  chirped, shadows of all previousness each
two in each other's embrace. She was a Safro-
  nia all her own, she said, not another name
           for

Ahdja, not a mask for Sophia, an abandon-
   ment of all of that, herself the abandoned
one. She felt her own to be a body of water no

                                             mat-
   ter, Lake Pred whose dread assistance we
enlisted, no most or more to be had... We were
   back in the Dread Lakes region it appeared.

                                          Was
      it Nur, was it Gat, was the question, the set-
   tler amendment put bullets everywhere. The
   land of a million names it might've been, Saf-
ronia's the only one stayed put, name none else

                                             than
   hers. Even so, we saw subversion everywhere
      but nothing subverted, a utopia nowhere to
be seen. As for me, I felt escorted into an arbor

                                              of
   atavai, ambient gods betrayed by the odor of
      linseed oil, totemic airlings again. Was it Nur,
was it Gat, was the question, all of us against the
   grain of it were it wood, would it were wood,

                                             all
   a way of looking away... So much I wanted
to stop wanting what I wanted was maybe all
   it was, so much I wanted not to see what I saw,

                                             the
   grand arcade of all that was, the most minus-
cule dip or degree. A capacious hangar held it
   all, a hangar whose environs the lakes were, the

                                          ar-
   mory the air now
was

·

So sweet a dream of attunement we were loath
　　to wake up, dreamt entwinement so sweet
　　we woke up weeping. Time whisking us away,
　　　　　　　　　　　　　　　　　　　　　　we

　　were the sensitive ones, no longer dark to be-
ing dark to ourselves, Nub's disconjugate gaze
　　pinned on us, put upon by thyroid storm. It got
　　　　　　　　　　　　　　　　　　　　　to

　　where all we wanted was to touch down light-
ly, a dream of utopian mesh whose demise we
　　went on grieving, an aleatory sacred we saw. It
　　　　　　　　　　　　　　　　　　　　was

　　a lover's question rage ran all the way thru…
As on a screen saw someone shot, the ghost of
　　all hope a new god over us, lord in whose care
we sank, stone more stone than stone. "Our lord
　　　　　　　　　　　　　　　　　　　who

　　don't like ugly" no longer, lord of the inland
sea we called bullet spray, lord whose nose filled
　　　　　　　　　　　　　　　　　　　　with

　　smoke

•

(diptych)

Devotional work they were of a mind to call
it, the way one mapped it out in one's head.
   They were the we we'd been but were done
                                             with,
   tremulous youth nothing if not squandered
money. We had rowed our way in from the
   Spite Islands, a trip long to be recounted
caught up in a myth of unlay, its ythm, a tune
                                             we
   played we stayed away from, played playing
   keep-away from... We sat in a house over-
looking Highway 60, eucalyptus flames housed
                                             in
   potentia all around. Again like a splurge or
like a barrage of lost money, again I awoke wish-
ing I knew. I lay imagining Andreannette's
                                             chur-
   chical girth and as quick was done with it,
bouquet put upon pungency, down doctrine
   up from inside... We sat ensconced inside
                                             eter-
nity's living room, bodily beauty the boon it
   was no matter. We sat bored outside time, way
                                             be-
   yond
tears

•

(diptych)

Devotional work they were of a mind to call
it, the way one mapped it out in one's head.
   They were the we we'd been but were done
                                          with,
   tremulous youth nothing if not squandered
money. We had rowed our way in from the
   Spite Islands, a trip long to be recounted
caught up in a myth of unlay, its ythm, a tune
                                          we
played we stayed away from, played playing
   keep-away from… We sat in a house over-
looking Highway 60, eucalyptus flames housed
                                          in
   potentia all around. Again like a splurge or
like a barrage of lost money, again I awoke wish-
   ing I knew. I lay imagining Andreannette's
                                          chur-
   chical girth and as quick was done with it,
bouquet put upon pungency, down doctrine
   up from inside… We sat ensconced inside
                                          eter-
nity's kitchen, bodily breakdown the bane it
   was no matter. We sat excited outside time,
                                          way
   beyond
tears

Pastor McDoubt stood at our beck, we of
the Newtown shrapnel, Nub's new church Nub's
new and old church, the belief so much was

                                    made
    of. God was liking ugly it seemed, God or
    God's ghost, what it was to see it so. A mi-
    grant allure maybe, vagrancy's rebuff... We

                        sat
in a room tucked away next to nowhere, empa-
    thy eggshell thin. Kleptocratic Nur, theft lorded
over us, frangible body, borne-away breath... I

                                heard
    my mother say she couldn't catch one, woke up

                                        wish-

    ing I
knew

"Way late," we said, chiming. Inside the
  moment, mentionless, we put more medi-
cine on the box and were gone again. We
                                        had
    broken camp and begun a promenade
  of the wounded, backed by a poorly played
  violin. Commencement time we called it,
                                        we
  the asymmetrics, we the malformed, making
    it moving on whatever way... Three parts
quarrel, four parts quiz, tattletale crows in the
                                        woods
    all around us, harps hung from the branches
  it seemed. Zvia's London charcoal dirtied our
  feet, entropic scraw of which we were there to
                                        be-
    stow a glimpse, what affray we were accord-
  ed by Lake Pred's yonder side. "Such affray
    as we were appointed," one heard the hovering
  dead complain, all to say they wanted not to've
                                        not
    been noticed, not to've not been talked about...
Chafing skin fell away leaving bones and moist
  organs. There was a we that was always moving.
                                        There
    was a we that only stood pat. Pomp orbited cir-
  cumstance even so. One put medicine on one's
    back, the pack one put it into the legendary hump-
backed flute-player's hump. A long bone ran thru
                                        one's
    head, boneheaded one already was no matter,
    woe folded in of itself, some stitched interstice,
knitting's preserve unstrung... We stood on Lake
                                        Pred's
    windy shore before we knew it, phosphores-
  cence a kind of capture we found our way by, the
    bone walls lit by particulate screams blowing,
                                        the
  going of the gone's res-
idue

●

The lit skull's premise reappeared. The sup-
   position it put away was not to be put away,
sugar what would once have been bone. We
                                stood
   looking out over Lake Pred, white breakers
lifted by the wind coming in. Lake Pred, a
   remarkable beast reputed to live therein, the
                           ap-
prentice prez's hurry-up summit elsewise in the
   air, an impending parade, an exfoliate sneeze…
It was all one to us whether or not it did, all one
                         weth-
er whatsay told it like it was, the way of telling
   and the way of was one. It was all one to us,
the unwieldy medicine on our backs, the choke
   bones caught in our throats coughed up, the fish
                       from
   the lake we ate. It was all the same to us, one
part cumin, two parts thyme, fishtail token of
   Nur's new aplomb, all the things we'd be all for
nought… I sank into my skin deep as I could. It
                   was
   all one and the same to me, the precessions of
Lake Pred, washed up anew as of an outpost of
                Mu,
   no such known
   outpost

We looked out on the lake wanting boats to
be on it, as if to embark was already to abide
   elsewhere, bodily elán stored away toward a
                                           far-
      away place. We were there but not there,
   notes read of late on how. It was all nothing to
   us whether we embarked or disembarked,
the giving away and the taking back taken deep.
                                           We
      stood recollecting Lorca's dark doves, braced
         against the bombs to come… "I saw my muse
   eat a sandwich in hell," said the trash-talking
                                           sun,
      "a dreamer's delight to be had beneath her
   light cotton smock." We stood looking. "A pear
   tree lived in by blackbirds," the trash-talking
                                           moon
      avowed, "lit my beloved's
   night"

•

The lake's exteriority lay secured, all husk,
   as it was, all there was anyway, nothing
nowhere near as much. Nur was the last gasp
                    of
    something. We knew what the something
  was. "Way late," we said, "no use blowing
  up," a desperate "Do something!" held back.
                Our
    broken camp infiltrated the air, a benign ab-
straction. A build-up of medicine coated our
   tongues and made them water. We were zon-
ing from inside out… Likelihood's perimeter
               lay
    surrounded, we saw ourselves inside our
would-be boat. Brother B came aboard finger-
popping, he broke his fingers he popped so
              hard.
Medicine hung heavy, a lengthening satchel
  on our backs, heavy on the box as well, "Con-
quistador." Brother B's popped-out fingers lay
             on
    the deck, all one to the Lake Pred boat wheth-
   er or not we embarked. To bask in the end
of things was our delight… Jittery winds made us
  list, adrift in the kairosphere, Andoumboulou
             al-
    beit the Dogon we'd known were none. It
was the boat of the dead we were on, would-be
   though it was, the something whose last gasp
it was, the throes whose paroxysm it was. Fits
            and
   starts come upon us like a chill, so abrupt we
   shook. We stood, still on the shore, watery
legs at lake's edge, torsos the boat we were in,
             the
    lowdown shame it was… Some same place
we went to it was, there but to be there again
   it seemed… Choppy water. Bumpy road… An
            er-
rand we were loath to
be on

We had journeyed from the town with a silly-
   sounding name, Tock City, the town clock
lulled us to sleep. Itamar stood hugging Zvia.

                                                Zvia
      said the lake was a mirage... Lake Pred
made of paint lay remaindering gloom, its the
      oldest book we knew. There was no such
place as Lake Pred, a certain side of each of us

                                                pro-
      claimed, all one to us whether or not there
was, we said, all one to us whether God liked ug-
   ly or not, all we needed was a line of horns...

                                                It
      was all one to us whether or not, all accru-
   ing to the one we gnosted more than knew, the

                                                over-
      ghost we we
   were

   Thus the morning after, Lake Pred's bod-
ily correlative a kind of reflux, Lake Pred
  nought if not a mirage. Whether all one or
                            all
   accruing to the one, the two of them one
  for a night… Zvia stood naked in the morning
  light, loins red where Itamar's mouth had
                        been,
  wiry hair where her legs met wet. Dilated
  in thought, his nose nudged her biscuit still,
that such as her thought not to have one had
                       one
   a marvel still… "Sweet biscuit," he almost
  whispered out loud, all the sweeter the more
  unlikely, likeliness a kind of finality, closure
                      he
  would not a-
bide

By which time what Lake Pred was had
    receded, a place a dead we, while alive, had
come thru. It wanted to say something about
                                            nerve
    church. Tremor bore on it as well. Some-
thing about seeming's degree… So much
    to do with "all one" and "all accruing to the
                                            one,"
    so much it put our heads on a swivel, so
much ado. The we we were lay buried so
    far inside we as well were not there, side
                                            ef-
fects or collateral damage, as one with Lake
                                            Pred
    not being
there

We backed away from the silly-sound-
  ing lake, Lake Pred, taken out look-
  ing at light's play on water. The book it
                    oth-
  erwise was or whose it was flared up
in green, the murmuring of jinns caught in
  the poplars and the silver dollar trees...
                  New
  inductees into the nerve church we were
  or we soon would be, goaded by horns,
pulled on by string, feet shod anew by batá
                   drums.
  It was all only we were at Carolina Beach,
    the bleak Atlantic, black bones up and
down the beach, Bone Coast we called it,
                 Fet-
  id Pond, Pred Lake. The Middle Passage
kept coming ashore... Some quick spot of
  love among the refuse intervened, Itamar
and Zvia, Brother B and Sister C, all the want
                 and
  the would-be blaring on boxes up and down
the sand, underness of no moment but what
  came forth was the underness of it, the book
                 of
  coming forth Pred otherwise was. Andre-
annette had said, "Direness no end," and so it
  seemed, underness other enough to itself to
                 roll
  the obvious in, the base it all built up from,
    Nub's inaugural affront... We stood put upon
by the rhyming jinns, the scattered bones were
                 so
  black they might've been made of tar, crabs'
claws took hold of our feet. *The silver dollar
trees' leaves,* the rhyme went, *like leaves of a*
                 ledg-
  er, misery's masquerade, the wind and all
else profiting nothing, nought if not a soul ser-

enade... Pred Pond was Pred Atlantic, Pred

At-

lantic Pred
Lake

Lake Pred was no lake but a precondition,
  predecessor assault that kept coming,
preterite arrest we couldn't quit. We were
                           each
    an unwieldy vessel it made us feel, rogue
boats all of us and of late all of us adrift.
  We bobbed athwart the we we'd be… It
                        was-
  n't our failing yet it was. It was all our
fault but it wasn't. So cut the waters of
Lake Pred, never not one thing but anoth-
er, always remanded again. "What exactly
                       I'm
    about" popped into my head and popped
out of my mouth, an it of which the we we'd
  be would have none… I saw my light lift
                      at
    last, I wanted to say as I balked, Pred's
name on my tongue like water on fish. What
  to do but let it be and be in it, canvassing
                     rest
  and irre-
gard

•

The jinns hummed upside down, feet tied
  to the sky, a weaving wind maybe all
it was but enough, being that, were being
                                        e-
  nough not moot. No way was it moot,
bones the lake's namesake took away. It was
  all only so much detritus history washed
                                        up,
    so much not known as history lest his-
  tory contain too much. In that light we
  scraped water on the wind, a quaint way
                                        of
writing, a way some took to be mimicking
  speech… It was a quaint way of writing,
not mimicking speech, no matter a kind of tap
                                        ran
    alongside. The jinns, we'd heard, held ham-
  mers. They made short work of time we'd
  often heard. So was our record tapped away
we'd been told. The realty-show prez had us
                                        de-
  pressed, toxic shock like never before… We
    were trying to make a place apart, klepto-
cratic bombardment we were insisting we could
  push back, we were trying to prepare a place.
                                        Aco-
    lytes in the nerve church, captive, "a mad-
man at the wheel" for real, we filled many a pew,
    the we we'd be, the spite vote no time soon to
                                        be
  gotten o-
over

The book's promise of eternity enshrined
    Lake Pred, a place that almost was, almost
  wasn't. It was the book thereof we spoke
                                        in-
    side, a people of the arrival whose thread-
  ing was Lake Pred, no eventual exit would
    there be... A weak eternity it turned out to
                                        be,
      brute extent or extenuation, no let-up's
    law. Love's coveted sashay had a way of
      receding, a predicate laid at arm's length, a
                                        pred-
  icate we backed away from, Lake Pred a cer-
    tain surge, the hour and the season such as
                                        they
    were

In my dream Lake Pred had been smaller.
　I walked its perimeter awaiting love
　with the woman of my dreams. A college
　　　　　　　　　　　　　　　　cam-
　　pus it felt like, a golden relapse, prede-
cessor complaint the stoic demand made
　on the living by the dead who were dying
　　　　　　　　　　　　　　　　　of
thirst… They were the dead and the living
　　dead, the living dead and the dead, the lake
　　　　　　　　　　　　　　　　held

　how much they'd've
drank

On this the short side of memory, a backed-
    into interiority held sway. Ocean. Pond.
  Lake. Lagoon. Exactly which it was was no
                                        mat-
    ter, the vicissitudes of appraising Lake Pred
      leaned in… We inside the nerve church
  on the verge of tears went on being beset, the
                                          ap-
    prentice prez at it again. Bones on cement-
  block floors, babies in cages, the nightmare
                                      we
      woke up
    in

ANUNCIO'S SIXTEENTH LAST LOVE SONG

—"mu" two hundred thirty-fifth part—

Anuncio's Osirian member lay lost or at
   large, a diffuse foray Anuncia's ass-
  cleft incited, her broad lower back and her

                        bur-
   geoning hips' invitation, the valley of
    sight descending to meet the unseen. Fer-
vency's own invite it seemed, pheromonal

                          musk,
   flags and flyovers crowding the sky over
Nur no matter, a last love song love's last
   resort... But the body he thought was his

                        was-
   n't, Anuncia warned, neither his nor hers.
They lay alive but living close to the dead,
   wondering were they dead or alive, that this
or that bodily gate make moan into music the

                        wish
   they lay there with. That vibrating body and
    bone keep Nur at bay was their wish... They
were beginning not to be able to breathe, wish

                        not-
   withstanding, wish no matter how stubborn
no matter, beginning to all fade away, the boon
   bodiliness had been. Scraps of memory hung

                        in
   the air, all there was, was's last recourse.
Scraps of melody they wanted to believe, the
   song whose allegory they were, out in the
world and back, song number four times four.

                       Song
   four squared the song they were they want-
    ed to believe, numeracy's day run come run,
whatever it was whatever it took... Four to the
   second... Two to the fourth... Figures whose

                       fig-
   ures they'd be... The doctrine of the end of
things was in their heads, no not knowing it,
   no getting away. Bodies were subtraction now.

                       All

it was was thread, yarn they spun, lore whose
propagation we egged on, chorusing nigh, re-
dundancy's choir we might've become though

                                        we

did

Anuncia's Isisian lap loomed like a pillow, a
   cloud he rested his head on, not-know he
took refuge in. Done-dead he lay, hand on
                                          her
      back, head on her belly, awoken by a
   dream that shook the bed. We the go-head
   choir saw the song whose allegory they
                                          were.
   We saw but could not sing it, lastloveness
      a kind of time we tried keeping but couldn't
keep, the lineaments of when an ythmic mien
                                          way
      beyond our
could

•

Line whose prolongation broke and began
    again, the meting out of which was the
song whose allegory they were, the song we
                                    saw,

    not sang. It came into view the way they
comported themselves, a wet kiss after which
    they rolled away and lay back to back and
                                    be-

        gan dreaming about a life after death. It
wasn't ours to say they were right or that
    they were wrong, Mrs. P reminded us, Mr.
                                    P

having dreamt it himself, she announced,
    Mr. P attesting it was so... I remembered a
dream of life before death I once dreamt, an
                                    aspi-

        ration southern Spain had to do with, the
    elsewhere music is had to do with, "had to
do with" holding a place a more precise turn
    would occupy. I saw my voice ring out to that
                                    ef-

    fect, saw but couldn't be said to be singing,
"had to do with" caught in my throat. It fell
    to the illustrative two to be the song we'd've
                                    sung,

        the last love we sang not singing, song long
since unspun... Anuncio and Anuncia's illus-
    trative manner spoke without speaking. Looking
on, we the would-be chorus did likewise. To be
                                    was

    to be seen and to be seen a kind of speaking.
    So, at least, the done-dead couple said without
speaking, last love's tease our testament, our
                                    wit-

    ness as well would-be, the done-dead conju-
gants back from the dead... Anuncio dozed
    off remembering, well met many years back,
                                    A-

    nuncia walking toward him, late afternoon,
New Mexico, out of nowhere he wanted to
    say but held back, so comely smoke rose off
                                    her

skin… All of it an abstract notelessness,
nonsonant testament told in sigil, indent, print

                                                   part-

   ing made on the
   wind

              •

   Anuncia loomed large atop a low ridge walk-
     ing toward Anuncio, body and face on fire.
  It was as it had been and would never be again,

                                                a

   last love song, another last love song, first-
  ness's ancillary track. It was as need fever's
   baton made its way inside the nerve church,

                                           bod-

    ily blush whose like would not be known
  again. It was bodily affection's requiem, freck-
   led face and bosom a requisite door not to be

                                       gone

   thru again, the putting away of which was the
   song or the song's intent… "Ready of not,"
  Anuncia said, "not ready," all the graces lit and

                                       gone

   before she spoke, another kind of speaking
   her descent from the ridge rose to the level
  of, contrary motion's gift… "Was it Steal-Away
  Ridge?" we asked Anuncio, New Mexico not

                                   hav-

   ing such history we knew or we thought we
  knew but asked ourselves who knew. Anuncio an-
  swered no and then answered yes. "Yes," he
  allowed, "loosely speaking," which by this time

                                   was

   the only kind there was, the sun's glow behind
    Anuncia mesmeric. So Steal-Away Ridge it
  was, the saying-so not saying so but up against it,

                                       think-

   ing that was all there was anyway, all there ever
  was… The far side of the ridge leaned in as we
   thought it, the beyond we thought, wishing we
  could. "Please, please, Mr. P," we begged, "tell

                                   us

the dream Mrs. P said you dreamt." The sun's
　　glow made the air an amber liqueur. "I dreamt
I tutored my sorrows in a school of mirage," Mr.
　　　　　　　　　　　　　　　　　　　　P

　　answered, "I dreamt I titrated the seen with the
seeming. I saw babies put in cages, I tutored my
　　despair in the school of oud. A mariachi maqam I
　　　　　　　　　　　　　　　　　　　　　was

　　made to play, a zafacaite taqsim," his way, it
　　seemed, of saying back off... We turned away, so
　　much else going on. The New Mexican mesa
turned blue the longer we thought it, looking out
　　　　　　　　　　　　　　　　　　　　thru

　　Anuncio's eyes. We were pulling away from
the world, as he was or he wished he were. Anun-
cia's walk toward him strapped him to it, the
　　　　　　　　　　　　　　　　　eng-

　　lish we lent him helpless, look thru his eyes
the way we did no matter, no matter we sat look-
　　ing leaning back. Done-dead was the lean we
　　　　　　　　　　　　　　　　　　of-

fered, chairs tilted on their back legs, a collective
　　Ghede asking what did loving make... We crossed
our legs leaning back no end, Anuncio sat with his
　　　　　　　　　　　　　　　　　un-

　　crossed, chair legs all on the floor. We crossed our
　　　　　　　　　　　　　　　　　　legs

　　leaning back to no
avail

Legendary love stood them up as we looked
   on. Late of an Egyptian manner, a Trinidadi-
an done-dead manner, ours was a notional

                                    ap-
   proach. The sublimity of it dug to a cer-
      tain key, a certain cunning, soon-come ag-
     grandizement ready or not no matter, the

                                      linea-
   ments of man-
ner itself

UNTITLED ORIGINAL 11386I

—"mu" two hundred thirty-sixth part—

As if I saw blood run down my neck, I
heard gurgling say, "Say something," the
blood. A fabled elsewhere the oud I played

       es-
poused, an elsewhere's elsewhere the dou-
ble strings contrived. I stood in the center
of an eight-pointed star, side-eyed... Soon

        it
seemed I schooled my oud on circumambi-
ence, a being-around or a being-about,
subject itself subject to qualm, semiquaver,

       com-
plaint. I was the abandoned boy asking
what not being would be like, all the more the
more no one could answer, what would not
being be like... At the moment of letting go

       one
would know, I was thinking, except not be-
ing there to know, except there being no one
to know. I was the abandoned boy again. Nur's
aggrieved whiteness gave me jitters. Why was it

       we
who got schooled on notness, I was asking, we
whose we-the-people fell flat, we their we-the-
people landed on, they their own migrating we.

       It
all bore me eastward, Trane at my side on so-
prano, waft so thick, the air so exact an attar,
we played our noses I thought... It was the dila-
tional sound of yore I knew and loved, dilational

       tone
and buzz, burr, bite. We played ignoring the
line between anywhere and somewhere. Noncos-
micity gave ground, ceded the way as we had

       our
way. Meant to charm snakes it might've been, so
open-throated I dreamt I bled. Next I knew
Leroy Jenkins joined us, bowing hard but going

       no-

where, a utopic "nowhere" run… We played
keeping history at bay or it was history was what
we played. No matter I sat in a cage, we played

                                    on

the line joining anywhere with somewhere, played
away the border between. I was in the school
of oud again, the abandoned boy wanting Nub's

                                    cray-

fish, fretless play all I could
eat

My oud a Nativity goose, Trane's horn part
   horn, part hookah, we played in a cage,
made to pledge allegiance. We were feeling
                                        hap-
      penstance's hand on our shoulders, the
we we'd be. We had taken a real trip, Trane
   was heard to say, on a real ship, no matter
                                          real
      seemed up in the air, the realty prez's way
      with fact what the matter was. We blew with
soup-cooler aplomb, unexcelled... Why the
                                        bent
      neck I wondered, looking at my oud. Was
      there just a record on the box I played along
with I wondered, fighting back toe cramps
                                       keep-
ing time with my foot. I wasn't fretless like
   before... The weave went on without me or
with me but ragged. Trane and Leroy said it
                                         was
   okay. Why the bent neck
   I went on wonder-
ing

•

Into the mystery it would come to be seen
as, the deejay librarian held sway in the school
of oud. A hollow block of wood, a wooden

                                egg
I sat holding, I was exactly an orphan now.
Sad cage they were calling freedom, cage
we shedded in. Empathetic Leroy, empathetic

                                 Trane
at the border, an empathetic serenade it seemed…
I played with an awkwardness they said was
true. An apt inability to advance Leroy called it, stu-
dent of "going nowhere" that he was. We were of

                                 an-
other we, he told me, subject to summary slaugh-
ter, each an emir of nothingness, an under-
ness lighting our way. Better my axe's neck than

                                 mine
I was thinking, the muse's hard look not unbe-
known to me… Bent necks were many I finally saw
it wanted to say, wrung necks of the lynched and

                                 of
the otherwise disappeared. I hung my head the
longer I played, neck bent à la Picasso, goose-
necked. Blue noose, blue gnosis, blue impromptu

                                 the
truth
was

It was Ohnedaruth's day again, truth be told,
   blue Trane, blue truth, dark light in a dark
time, bent necks bent but not broke. Not to not
                                        men-
   tion Elvin knocking underneath, off to one
side. Song in a strange land long since, how now
   not to sing except to sing tear it all a brand
                                        new...
   It was Ohnedaruth's day again, Leroy
brought in for the extension string meant, his
   and mine and Jimmy's Hofriyati thread. It
                                        was

Ohnedaruth's day rebe-
gun

No matter what else, I needed, like Wayne
said, not to think about music. I called
on thoughts of the hair within my lady's love
                                        re-
    gion, a koan of sorts, her ladyship such
as it was, nothing less likely there... I feasted
    on paradox, of a mind for what was not,
                                        wide-
eyed for what would not be seen, a late les-
    son in notness grown motivic, a school of
                                        di-
    lation a-
gain

No neck bent but whose it no longer
was was me and my oud's dream of
success. Ovoid back more belly than

                                    back,
    not not to mention its rhyme with
    jelly. A mystic remit we tested our teeth

                                    with…

    Madrigal briar,
breath

All hands were on deck as we docked
in the nerve church, metaphoric boat
  of soul metamorphic, boat-shaped back
                                    of

  the oud whose belly we rode in, ety-
mologic boat of soul catastrophic, church
  whose nave we were in. Church cast-
ing color cast a stain on the world. It bore
                                  the

  bright light we'd been thru, gone round
and come thru again, metamorphic boat
  of soul metaphoric, of what no one would
                                say...

  Whatever it was was what soul was, of
which only the asker wanted to know.
  All hands were on deck even so. All had
                          gone

  well were it only body nerve church meant,
    well were it only soul it meant, well were
it not a thread of the two, other than either, a
                              thread

    and a third, off to itself. All had gone well
  that way, would've gone well were it the way,
    way that it wasn't, would that it were... We
                                lay

    held in the oud whose belly was black, all
  hands on deck as we docked, bent neck and
    bent knee de rigueur in the nerve church, co-
  nundrum the head it hit. Meat and bone apart
                              from

    meat and bone was the nerve church, soul
  unbeknown to itself it also was, a certain some-
    thing not something notwithstanding, asked
                              a-

bout no matter no answer would accrue. All
    hands were on deck proclaiming soul, soul not
  something to be said to be had, soul that was
                              a

    boat and that sat in the boat it was, borne
  beknown to itself. All hands were on deck not

proclaiming soul. The less we boasted the
                                    bet-
ter we rode the boat that soul was, the boat that
                                    sold
    us thought to be that
    boat

                    .

Some were said to have limbo'd below deck,
    the lute's dark insides a madrigal of sorts, its
back less back than belly. Some were said to
                                    have
    bent back while surrounded by singers, bent
back so far their heads were on the floor. The
    backs of their heads were on the floor, it was
                                    said,
    brushed it, the back of the head a belly di-
gesting damage, no way its way a way… Some
    were said, once on deck, to have jumped, a
shark's teeth or breathlessness the way, no way,
                                    was
    theirs, jumped, some said, or were thrown. We
    knew all this coming into the nerve church, its
nave encyclopedic, no outrage not written down,
                                    histo-
    ry a parable of nerve, who
    had it

Huff sat at the wheel of the bus calling it a
boat. We were leaving Low Forest again,
   a sea of green he called it, all aboard as he

                                    now
called the bus a train. Eleanoir's blue truck
   it might've been, might well have been,
   might as well have been, so metamorphic the

                                    dock
   whence we embarked… It was nothing if
not Eleanoir's dream, the ship we were in, lute
   of the light-lady of night, Eleanoir's loot, we

                                    sur-
   mised. Not since primordial beak met pri-
   mordial seed had it so accrued, no mile not
   haunted, no matter what move we made. Our

                                    bus
   put-putted a-
long

A canopy of leaves overhead as we made
our way, the sea of green Huff insisted we
  call it, the bus our boat and all of it the nerve
                                 church,
    nothing not inflected by the blood-guzzling
lute whose intestines history was. Wagadu
  lay within sight even so, it or the Eleven Light
City, Eleanoir sitting behind the driver's seat,
                            whis-
    pering things in Huff's ear... Eleanoir and
Huff we'd have never thought but there it was,
  Huff under Eleanoir's influence, Eleanoir
                      un-
    der his. A boat their bed would be we
heard him whisper back, his and her wish as
  much ours as theirs, that history give way
                        to
romance, what lit the nerve church. Our bus
  bumped along, vestiges of memory afoot, de-
bris the boat of soul grew laden with, the lute
                        our
    boat also was claiming blood... The school
  of oud instructed us, taught with drawn strings,
taut cartilage and sinew also known as nerve
  church, our tutorial wherein, we saw, would no
                        time
    soon recess. Eleanoir's face, which had float-
ed many a boat, now floated Huff's it came clear
  for us to see, nerve church, whose nave we
docked in, nuptial perhaps, our notional romance
                        call-
  ing history moot, such the way we got by...
Such the way we got by proved everyday by soul
  music Brother B said. Peaches and Herb had
                        come
  on the box. A metaphoric love boat the meta-
morpic boat of soul turned into now. We were
  on our way who knew where, bus, boat, train or
                        truck,
  on our way wherever, soon
come

·

We felt the press of consequence inside the
nerve church, the lute's underbelly the oud,
   the madrig's underbelly the panther, the deck's

                                un-

   derbelly the hold, metamorphic soul's under-
belly foreboding. We were far from Low For-
   est now, far from Lone Coast, on a train from

                               Bar-

   celona to Lyon. Eleanoir slept lying across the
   seat across from Itamar and me, her head on
Huff's lap. Her small feet peeped out beautifully

                            from

   under the blanket she lay wrapped up in… The
   train was a boat or it would take us to a boat,
unclear which, the boat of soul that lay docked in the
   nerve church, all hands on deck awaiting us, if not,

                            ac-

   cording to some, none other than us. It was night,
nothing visible outside our windows. The commis-
   erative dead gauged our quotient of soul, no one able
to say what it was though we rode it, the riding alone

                         was

   clear… The train ran away with us, took us away,
   soul riding us it seemed, warm and humid with the
breath and the breathing of bodies, a blind winding

                       or

   a boat finding its way thru the night. There was
no way to know it but by its effects, Itamar was say-
ing, an array of aromas we took to pertain thereto

                        per-

   vading our
   car

Voices fell from the sky, never not
   inflected by the dead on the sea floor,
the dead under leaf, needle and cone in
                                 Low
   Forest, the dead and how they came
  to be that way, everywhere…They spoke
  of this as the bus rattled on, the boat
                              cut
thru water, the truck struggled going
  up a mountain, the train cried arkestral,
soul bumped again and again against
                            what
  would not
have it

ELEANOIR AND HUFF'S NEW BLUES AND GOSPEL

—"mu" two hundred thirty-eighth part—

The air lay lit with a kind of dread. Expec-
tancy's arraignment it felt like, the oud's
   outer inurement all there was, inside out.
                                             The
   conundrum the backs of our heads hit
was death. We thought of it the least often
   we could but a lot, the closer walk being
                                          what
it was. "Rue not the day," we'd been told…
Happenstance rode us like an orisha, the
unawares heaven we were in without knowing
                                             it
   almost to be beheld, recession a kind of res-
   cue, not to be held on to. A kind of circling
it seemed or it was we could not find a way
                                          out
of. Huff and Eleanoir, sudden lovers, caught
   unawares was only part of it, verities pur-
   veyed in a row the least part of it, the it whose
                                             it
   we would be… We stared out our windows,
Low Forest green a cathedral. Leafed limbs hung
   over us as we rode and were ridden, the green
                                          com-
   edy said by some to be clear profusion. The
dry cliffs of Bandiagara were a far cry away but
   we might've been underwater crossing Mu,
Huff so wanted it so. It was he who breathed life
                                             in-
to it all he'd've had us believe, the wobbly cap-
   tain who steered our boat a god decked out in
shades dark enough to blind. One saw the passion
                                          and
   the pathos of it, Huff's pathetic boast backed
   by someone inside each of us hollering would it
were his, would he had his way, someone inside
                                          Elea-
   noir the most, the bodies they newly saw they

wouldn't always have now newly poignant, lit
   with a new appeal… It was all creation myth,
creation ythm, by now, Sophia said, was but hadn't
                                           al-
   ways been. How to break free of the said she impli-
   citly asked, whatsay's world dominion, silence
long since no option, the underwater tissue of leaves
                                           we
   drove thru. She was the wise one, ever the one
     we'd heard of, always our luck to hear from. She
pressed her lips together, soft wrinkly flesh nixing
                                      talk,
   nixing kissing, adjourning all surrounding sound…
We were on Cornwallis, passing under 15-501, the
   daily for the moment immortal, preserved in amber,
                                     what-
   said lag let
  go

       •

   Ythm was a corollary life riding with us, a concur-
rency, a wrinkle in time. Accompaniment it could
   also be called and Sophia called it that, the green in
                                      the
   blue, the blue in the green… Not since embou-
   chure met nerve-end had it been so close to see, so
   wise or so conducing to wisdom we pounded the
                                    heels
of our hands together, pressed our tongues to the
   backs of our teeth… It was all one to us whether we
   came or we went, mythic or mystic the ythmic ride
                                  was,
   drained or adjoining Mu we
trekked

       •

So too with Huff and Eleanoir's romance, the
   lens they slew history with or made it with
history with, made history with. It was history
                                cut
   down to size. "Let us never put forth any-

thing unless it be parcel, part," Eleanoir had
said. "Breath and light beyond any before,"

                                    Huff
    had said, "bodily breakdown bear me thru."
So much of it was they wanted to speak that
    way, so much emotion a pretext for whatsay,

                              So-
phia would've said had she not summarily ad-
    journed all sound... It was a moment under
the overpass, traffic noise cancelled as well as all

                                    else,
    more than a philosophical pause but also that,
    a nonsonance none but Sophia knew was there.
Whatsay's collapse into nonsay rode with us now,
    momentary though the muting had been, return

                              to
    sonance though we did, nonsay itself the blue
vessel we bore thru green in. We rode along saying
    nothing now. It was all a corridor of green leaves

                              and
    light, the standing-pat of trees between which
we once debated if God could lie. We sat now
    tasting our tongues... All effortlessness it was now
or it seemed. Everything attested its place without

                                    call
    or complaint, "mu" as in mute, made clear. I
too sat tasting my tongue, Nub's descent into Nur
    a kind of coating, nothing not affected by Nub's

                                    un-
    mer-
cy

The trees were breathing in and breathing out
   for us, transitory support we rode on.
The realty show was depleting Low Forest
                 and
   we cruised anyway, an ambiguous boat
    amid a sea of green. "We took a real trip,"
Trane had said, "on a real ship," imaginary
               sound
   more real than the wind riffling the leaves,
the hum of rubber on asphalt, the ones that
   were there… A faint, far eastern keening had
                one's
   ear, Nub's descent into Nur a kind of croon
it prevailed against, hatesay remanding the
   we we'd be, "mu" as in moot. Turned away,
              we
   rode our boat of longing, locked out of the hea-
    ven we'd been in not knowing we were in it,
             immi-
   grant wish the boat we
rode

•

It was Huff who had called it all myth, all ythm,
   a clipped or some other way compromised
rhythm. There was an imaginal sound, he said,
                    loud-

   er than sound we could hear, boat of soul
the school of oud, oud as old as wood some said,
   some said even older. With this wood's daugh-
ter Eleanoir took issue, wood not to be said to
                  have

   come later, she said, subsequent to the oud's
   pear shape, the pear not possibly prior to
the tree that bore it. Shape, she went on, was no
              ab-

   straction, shape was even less possibly prior.
   "Enough with the 'some,'" she said. "What do you
   say?" she asked… It was the beginning of he-
said-she-said, cosmogonic wuh rebutted by cosmic
              flirt,

   things began to come apart. "Wood was less it-
self before oud was," Huff answered. "Oud is what
   made wood matter, oud itself more virtual than
             real,

   especially the school of it. Oud is only illuso-
rily matter, imaginal sound beyond concrete
   audition." Wood's daughter, whose dream, af-
ter all, it was we were in, her dream of the blue
            truck

   that might've been a bus, might've been a boat,
   said little. "Wood is wood," Eleanoir said. Then
she said no more, said nothing, not-saying saying
             more

   than saying would. "Trouble ahead," Ahdja whis-
   pered in my ear… Huff himself not knowing,
Eleanoir had no way of knowing eucalyptus trunks
             bare

   of their bark were a Lone Coast memory, a grove
of them Huff's dream, his blue remit. A long way
   away and a long way back. He spoke of wood as
            one

   who spoke of flesh, as of a grove of legs, bark
stripped away showing loinlike whiteness under-

neath, a Greco-arboreal mytheme or ythmeme,
"leaves" informed of which he'd long read. Oud, she
                                                    had
   no way of knowing, he himself not knowing, was
      a transposition eastward, troubadour stuff, court-
ly legs he saw, dreaming westward, an erotico-ecologi-
   cal polis he saw proposed by the worry lines on her
                                                    face...
   How Eleanoir dreamt her not knowing, how dream
could specify what she didn't know without inform-
   ing her, none of us knew. How she dreamt Huff's not
                                                    know-
      ing we could see. Her dream was to know with-
   out knowing and to know more than he knew. Ahdja
      whispered all this to me... We ambled along leav-
ing the philosophic nonsonance behind, the overpass
                                                    be-
   hind, wood's daughter's falling silent of a piece with
      it though we cruised away, blue truck, blue bus,
blue boat, whatever it was we rode on or in, heroines
                                                    and
   heroes of her dreamt
récit

All hands were on deck as we exited the
   nerve church. We saw there was nothing
not stained with motion. The animate
                                    out-
   cry "We've been had" echoed all thru
the trees… Eleanoir and Huff, having fallen
   in, were now falling out, the pathos their
                                    would-
     be polis aroused gone against polis itself…
   A bare limning taking place took the place
    of the solid as their chances grew long,
                            they
   and we the fools it took turning wary, more
                                likely

    to've been trawling
sleep

Eleanoir and Huff served as a marker, their con-
juncture an imaginal sound no sound could
equal. It was an unkept, unkeepable promise, an
                                                un-
   keepable secret as well, the sound of words
on a page. We had gone wordless at the appren-
tice prez's antics, albeit much deeper was
                                          what
   was hitting the fan. The top was only the
tip, no matter how wide it spread. We worked
hard remembering that, Nub gone into Nur
                                         wide-
eyed where it was going, Nub's collapse into
   Nur the one-third wanted, a line crossed, cross-
es burned again... Words had held forth in the
                                             nerve
   church and they held forth now, held forth a-
gain, words on the tips of our tongues and on
   the tips of other tongues, other tongues on the
                                                 tips
   of our tongues. The imaginal sound no sound
could match kept at us, Nur the noise despite
   which we took our stab at living, hate afoot noth-
ing new. Nub stubs its toe from time to time we
                                               knew,
   maybe all the time. "Let's call it Stub," Itamar
let out, wording up. We put some music from Zan-
zibar on the box but took it off, not enough oud.
                                               We
   were the school of oud, school of Udhra, the
fools it took to learn, anything but the monied
   ones. "Con amor todo se puede," we said, semi-
said, semisang... We each felt an oud's back or
                                               belly
   against our abdomen, could each feel it verg-
      ing on ribcage theater. Our vehicular ambigu-
ity bothered us not at all. The dead rode with
                                               us,

never not there, just as we, when dead, would
never not be there. The dead's legendary thirst
was the imaginal sound no sound could match,

                                                syn-
  aesthetic the best we could do trying to speak
of it, the sound we were driven by. The dead's
  legendary thirst made us bedouins, lips chapped
no matter the green of Low Forest, the beloved's

                                               lips
  likewise dry... Otherwise we were silent, true
Pythagoreans, as if we'd been asked about the
  square root of two, sixty-five times two to the

                                             sec-
  ond all we'd say about number, be under or
inside more what it was than say. It was song six-
  ty-five times four we were in or were under,

                                            bent
  tautological figure, self-reflex, number the
letter it was. So it was we kissed like we were
  thirsty when we did, incendiary no matter it was,
tongue a jet of flame no matter. We wanted to be

                                           fools
  in Stub, where not to be was to prey on the world...
  Eleanoir and Huff had faded back into the we
we'd be, absorbed, reabsorbed, back to as they'd
 been before, the literalness of number never more

                                         irrel-
  evant, a feeling for the none what obtained. They
knew a philosophical readiness riding the curve
  of the belly or back the boat of soul we'd boarded

                                         was,
  a feeling for the none no one in Nub, Nur, Stub
wanted to know it was running from. We sought
  what solace there was looking out at the varieties

                                           of
green to be seen in Low For-
est

A feeling for the none seemed to accrue as we
motored on. Mock transit it might've been. We
saw a deer carcass picked at by buzzards on the

                                      side
  of the road. "See them as musicians," Ahdja
remarked, looking out her window, "see them
  as playing the oud, the way their beaks pull at

                                     the
  carcass a music we can see but not hear." We
indeed did see the none of it, buzzard beaks a
  barrage of plectra, ligament and sinew the strings
plucked and picked. The buzzards were hands and

                                    fingers
  whose play grew labored, a divine or demonic
  vehemence made a music we almost heard.
Hawks rendered the sky another Pred Lake, Low

                                    For-
  est a kind of heaven an-
yway

●

All accruing to the none we knew and bore
  knowing. Was polis only a part of that, we
wondered, the law of selection an election
                            taken
  away, an outpost on Pred Lake. Elegiac
  roost, elegiac witness, elegy what told us
what time it was, foothold fallen away or
                            taken
  away if not fallen, carcass on the side of
the road… The putrid music Ahdja made
us imagine was not the imaginal sound. A
                      rib-
  cage harmonics attended it all, so sad we
laughed in self-defense. An allegorical cast we
  thought it might get, events of which we
                      were
the terms, the meaning, each an attribute's
  embodiment albeit none of us could say ex-
actly which. An insensate chill came over
                    ev-
  erything, hot, humid day though it was.
  The deer's ribcage chimed a comedic air,
divine-comedic air. Never had Low Forest
  resounded so… We bumped along, happy to
                    have
  air to breathe, the green leaves doing their
job, lungs for a time healthy, all of us eventual-
  ly none. Scraps of memory rode what breeze
                  there
  was, chill sonority real but abstract. Scraps
of melody they might have been as well were we
  to hear again, we put *Live at the Village Van-*
guard Again! on. Pharoah's gruff butterfly brought
                  us
  back. We were back among the big trees, we
were back on Lone Coast, we were hearing with a
  hearing inside our heads and anywhere else. It
                got
heavy holding the world in our heads, our bus our
  boat. Our bus was a boat of longing, watery as
                the

sea we were
on

•

The boat of longing a boat of water, we sank,
    watery limbs the like of the roots undergirding
Low Forest, the all so much the none it shook
                                                us,
    watery ligament, cartilage, muscle, bone,
skin. Andreannette's ex's pea coat floated
    above her, she led our surfacing, back, lower
back and buttocks pear-shaped, bodily allure
                                        low-
    hanging fruit. Sophia reached and the rest
of us followed suit, reached and went on reach-
ing… Merpeople we were not but might've
                                        been.
    It was the wateriness of a kiss and much
more, a kind of drowning, the what-if and the
as-if again, ongoing, words on the tips of
                                        our
tongues and the tips of other tongues, other
    tongues on the tips of our tongues, the tip of
the beloved's tongue all there was, all there
                                        ever
was, any-
way

•

We lay absorbed in our moment, absorbed in
   our time, what but moment's gnosis none of us
could say. We lay in a ditch after the bus rolled

                                            over
      it seemed. Not all was well in the world of
         tone but the imaginal sound surfeit got us thru.
      The underwater sense persisted, floating gar-
         ments a kind of canopy blocking the sun… The

                                            boun-
      ty of limbs and torsos all incumbency, our hea-
      ven had been on earth, as had our hell. The sunken
      boat our bus had become was my body I felt,

                                       ra-
diated muscle gone fibrotic in my hip and thigh.
      The boon bodies were remained evident no mat-
      ter, a kind of self-evident, such the matter only

                                            with
         mine… What light came thru showed backs,
      lower backs and buttocks I was made helpless by,
         an otherwise invisible order I heard or I'd heard

                                            word
      of. What one saw one saw refracted, light bent at
      an angle a kind of lever, leverage what one needed
getting by. We were back in the school of oud was

                                            all
      it was, the oud's back the hull of a ship. Thus
      the beloved's lips' tutorial, all only so much accru-
         ing to the none, a nonce or an anodyne deliver-
      ance, rescue what proffer again… A proxy God we

                                            gave
      the name Go Head had our backs, wayfare for-
      ever though we might or most likely would. It was
      all one to us whether one or the other, womanly

                                            or
manly allure throughout the premises, water's re-
      turn to itself. We had gone back to primary form,
form assuming the shape of its retention, when and

                                            were
      there such, each, every and all. That or it was all
         in my mind or mostly, Brown vs. Bardo again,
   a dream such as the frog dream, a dream or a drifting

off, all the green gone blue before I knew it… The

                                                    truth

was our bus remained upright and we whizzed along,
    15-501 and 101, Lone Coast and Low Forest, the
ride, I wanted to say, of my life. All was accruing to

                                             noth-

ing as we rode, the school of the oud's back our
school of the wrought belly, Eleanoir and Huff a grade
    or degree thereof, ever not without a sexual aspect,

                                              wet-

ness and waft where their legs met, we the would-
be fools it took to learn. A school of the duck's back it
    also was, love's or the beloved's tutelage not to be
lost, water's first rolling away a dare to behold, all only

                                                so

much bluff. We were of the order of the dry feather,
don't-care acolytes. "Tear it up," we were time and
    again heard to say… "Not since," I wanted to say but

                                              not

since what wasn't evident yet. Tree after tree went
by outside my window, green back to green again.
    "Not since Andreannette's maidenly look wearing a

                                             pea

coat" came out at last, muse or madonna come into
    counterpoint with the carcass on the side of the road,
    the muse or madonna thumbing a ride. There was

                                            some-

thing it wanted to say about ride or to say using ride,
    something like we'd ride out the wretchedness of Nur,
something like we'd survive, that Go Head don't like

                                             ugly

    for long… It had to do with a call or a calm come
from beyond or behind visible extent. It wanted to say
    keep speaking thru love's irrelevant lips, to and with the
beloved's irrelevant tongue, to and upon the tip of the

                                             be-

loved's tongue. It was saying late love saw one thru,
would see us thru. It spoke of repossession by spirals, a late
word for spirit, it said, having-to-do-with a late word too.

                                              We

    rode along, riding along. We gazed out our windows,
we looked out at Low Forest, so much of which we could

                                             not

see

A lever let it be or let us call it, we resolved,
   the eventual pneumatic exit a kind of incline.
The boat of longing lifted our hands up over
                                      our
   heads, the clothes we wore stripped away,
floating above us. "Naked as jaybirds," the
   voiceover said. It felt good to be birds again…
                                      Our
dream was to be longer with our strained ekphras-
   tic state, the seen so digested imaginal sound
   upended heaven, carcass reverb audited for days…
                                        It
   was extolling the muse memory could be, the bits
of it riding the breeze a distended epic, dislocated
   this, dislocated that ramified forever, no such it as
                                    only

   once or
one